3-INGREDIENT COCKTAILS

3-INGREDIENT COCKTAILS

AN OPINIONATED GUIDE TO THE MOST ENDURING DRINKS IN THE COCKTAIL CANON

ROBERT SIMONSON

PHOTOGRAPHS BY COLIN PRICE

TEN SPEED PRESS
California | New York

ALSO BY ROBERT SIMONSON

The Old-Fashioned: The World's First Classic Cocktail, with Recipes and Lore

A Proper Drink: How a Band of Bartenders Saved the Civilized Drinking World

Published in the United States by Ten Speed Press, an imprint of the Crown
Publishing Group, a division of Penguin Random House LLC, New York.
www.crownpublishing.com
www.tenspeed.com

Ten Speed Press and the Ten Speed Press colophon are registered trademarks
of Penguin Random House LLC.

Portions of the section on the Gibson first appeared, in slightly different form,
in *Grub Street*.

Portions of the sections on the Mint Julep and Sidecar first appeared, in slightly
different form, in *Punch*.

Portions of the section on the Daiquiri first appeared, in slightly different form,
in *Saveur*.

Library of Congress Cataloging-in-Publication Data
Names: Simonson, Robert, author.
Title: Three-ingredient cocktails : an opinionated guide to the most enduring
    drinks in the cocktail canon / Robert Simonson ; photography by Colin Price.
Description: First edition. | California : Ten Speed Press, [2017] | Includes index.
Identifiers: LCCN 2017016197 | ISBN 9780399578540 (hardcover) |
    ISBN 9780399578557 (ebook)
Subjects: LCSH: Cocktails. | LCGFT: Cookbooks.
Classification: LCC TX951 .S5836 2017 | DDC 641.87/4--dc23
LC record available at https://lccn.loc.gov/2017016197

Hardcover ISBN: 978-0-399-57854-0
eBook ISBN: 978-0-399-57855-7

Printed in China

Design by Betsy Stromberg
Cover design by George Carpenter
Cover illustration by Matthew Allen
Drink styling by Emily Caneer
Prop styling by Glenn Jenkins

10 9 8 7 6 5 4 3

First Edition

Dedicated to
Mary Kate Murray

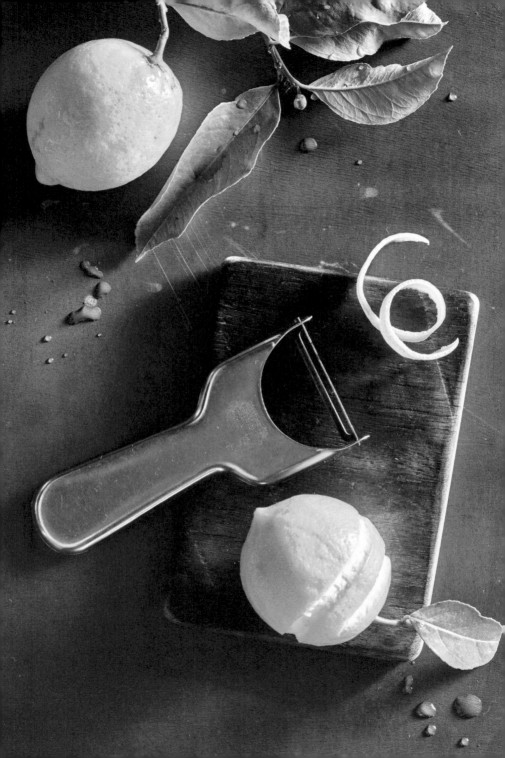

contents

Drinks

OLD-FASHIONED COCKTAILS

IMPROVED COCKTAILS

SOURS

HIGHBALLS

OTHER COCKTAILS

Introduction

You need three ingredients for a cocktail. Vodka and Mountain Dew is an emergency.
—PEGGY OLSON, *Mad Men*

Three—it's a magic number.

We see in three dimensions. Three strikes, you're out. Three-pointers are the highlight of any basketball game. Baby makes three. Reading, writing, and 'rithmatic makes an education. Three is a hat trick. Three's a charm. Ready, set, go. One, two, three: take the picture. Nobody counts to two. Nobody counts to four. Three makes magic.

The triangle is the most stable of shapes, so it comes as no surprise, then, that the three-ingredient cocktail is the most sturdy and lasting of cocktail constructions. One ingredient, you've got a nice dram. Two, you've got a highball. Get three things to marry together, you've likely got a cocktail on your hands. More than three and you've got a more complicated cocktail, not necessarily a better one.

Since the cocktail renaissance began around the turn of the twenty-first century, detractors have been complaining that too many of the new drinks being turned out by mixologists contain a surfeit of ingredients. "So what?" I often thought. If it leads to deliciousness, who cares if they threw in the kitchen sink and a pair of cufflinks?

Except, those detractors had a point. Complexity may lead to the flattery of the senses, but not to imitation. If the Manhattan had eight ingredients, nobody would be making it today—at least, not at home and probably not at many bars. There is practicality in the three-ingredient cocktail. Because you don't need a grocery cart when shopping for its fixin's at the liquor store, if it's tasty, it will catch on. Whiskey, vermouth, bitters? You got this.

There's also honesty in the three-ingredient cocktail. When you get past five ingredients in a drink, the further additives are often there, not to add to what's already present in the glass, but to correct what's still lacking in the mixture. If you spot a drink on a menu that has seven or eight things in it, chances are two of those are Band-Aids, attempting to mend a broken cocktail. That's not possible with a trio. There are no obfuscating ingredients the purpose of which might be to cloud the drinker's mind and mask some innate unsoundness of the drink. You can clearly taste and adjudge every component. Every player must be strong. As bartender Audrey Saunders once said, "The three-ingredient cocktail doesn't lie."

Finally, the three-ingredient cocktail has history on its side. Every time the cocktail world has stirred up dust within the great culture, it's because some three-legged liquid creature has ventured, all big-footed, onto the world's Main Street: the Whiskey Cocktail, Mint Julep, Manhattan, Martini, Tom Collins, Whiskey Sour, Daiquiri, Margarita, Moscow Mule, Negroni, and Harvey Wallbanger—all three-ingredient game-changers. Triumphal triptych cocktails don't provoke arguments about whether they're good or not; they start arguments about the best way to make them well. It's taken as an article of faith that they're good.

This is all a lot of words to justify something that doesn't really need justifying. Most everyone agrees there is some innate virtue in simplicity, whatever field of endeavor you're talking about. If you don't even agree to that, that's fine—contrary away. I'm the first to admit, in terms of cocktails, that it's possible to make a fairly solid argument for any style or method you choose to get behind. Think more is more? A lot of tiki drink aficionados would agree with you. Think that sous vide method brings out the flavor more strongly? Science has a case to make. I grant you all your points.

But this remains: these drinks are easy to make (point one), while none of them read on the tongue as simple-minded creations (point two), and they all taste good (point three). Give me an argument against that.

People often ask me what cocktails I make when I drink at home. The answer is, by and large, the ones included in these pages, the classics: Old-Fashioned, Manhattan, Daiquiri, Negroni, and so on. I turn to them regularly because they are delicious, dependable, and easy to prepare, and I almost always have the ingredients on hand. And if that is the situation for me, there's no reason it can't be the same with anyone reading this sentence. That was one reason for my writing this book. Another is that many of the cocktail books that have come out in recent years have been a little, well, fussy. Those volumes, put out by estimable bars and bartenders, all have something to offer. But perhaps this book can serve as an alternative.

While most of the cocktails that follow are well established and were invented decades ago, there are a number of new drinks. Finding those was more difficult, simply because hitting upon a solid, three-ingredient cocktail today is a tall order; most of the obvious formulae were laid down long ago. Still, I found a few worthy specimens of recent vintage.

Enough preamble—let's move on to the drinks—with some history and opinion woven through.

A Note on the Recipes

Most three-ingredient drinks can be divided into two camps: (1) spirit, sweetener, bitters; and (2) spirit, sweetener, citrus—better known as "sours." The former are, generally speaking, the stiff customers; the latter, the piquant refreshers.

For the purposes of this book, we've divided the recipes into five sections: Old-Fashioned Cocktails, based on the ur-cocktail formula from the nineteenth century of spirit, bitters, and sugar; "Improved Cocktails," an old term from the 1800s that refers to drinks that have been enhanced in one way or another by additional ingredients; Sours (see above); Highballs, for drinks that are served long and light; and Other Cocktails, a catchall category for all drinks that don't fit under the other four headings. Peppered throughout are short essays on drinks old and august enough to merit the essay treatment.

Keep in mind that when I say "sweetener," I'm not always talking sugar. It could be anything from sweet vermouth to liqueurs like Curaçao to syrups like grenadine to various types of soda. The "bitters," meanwhile, could be the kind dashed out of little bottles (as in the Angostura bitters in a Manhattan) or the bracing kinds made in Italy and found in big bottles (the Campari needed for a Negroni).

There are exceptions, of course. The Martini—spirit, modifier, bitters—is rather in a category all its own. All three ingredients combined produce something as dry as the Sahara. The Champagne Cocktail, meanwhile, has bitters and sugar, but calls for sparkling wine instead of a spirit, the modification bringing about the sort of swellegant change in personality you might expect.

Sticklers will point out that, for all the cocktails mentioned above, there is a phantom fourth ingredient: water. Just as you can't cook a steak without heat, you can't make a cocktail without water (first introduced in its frozen state but, through stirring and shaking, quickly insinuating itself into the recipe in liquid form). However, in this book, we're taking water for granted and focusing on beverage alcohol, sweeteners, juices, sodas, and bitters when we're counting up to three.

Similarly, garnishes don't count in my calculations. That is not to say they are not important; they are, in fact, critical to the finishing of many drinks. Want a Manhattan without a cherry? An Old-Fashioned without a twist? I didn't think so. But we're talking the solids and nonsolids that are in the glass before the creation gets crowned by a twist, an onion, an olive, a pineapple spear, or what have you. The suit; not the hat.

Equipment and Syrups

Though the recipes that follow are all simple, you need a fair-sized armory of bar equipment to make them. A run-down of the needed tools follows.

EQUIPMENT

A Boston shaker. This two-piece shaker, composed of a standard mixing glass and a metal mixing tin, is suitable for stirred drinks (for which you only need the mixing glass) and shaken drinks (for which you require both parts).

A bar spoon. A long bar spoon (approximately 11 inches) is needed for all stirred drinks.

A jigger. Most jiggers are stainless steel and have a dual-measure design. The most common ones have a 1-ounce capacity on one end and a ½-ounce capacity on the other; or a 1½-, ¾-ounce setup. It's good to have one of each to ensure accurate measurements.

Strainers. You need a julep strainer (which has a perforated bowl shape) for stirred drinks and a Hawthorne strainer (which has a metal coil wrapped around its bowl to keep out citrus pulp) for shaken drinks. The Hawthorne can do double duty if need be.

A muddler. You need a muddler for certain drinks that require you to mash up fruits, herbs, or sugar cubes at the bottom of a mixing glass or serving glass. Old-fashioned wooden specimens work best.

Large-scale ice trays. A large ice cube makes a big difference, both aesthetically and tastewise, in some stirred, sipping drinks, like the Old-Fashioned. Molds for these sorts of cubes, typically 2 by 2 inches in size, are now very easy to find.

SYRUPS

Many drinks call for simple syrup, which is nothing more than sugar water. The main difference between syrups is the proportion of sugar to water. Higher ratios of sugar make for a richer syrup, which leads to a richer mouthfeel for the cocktail. Following are the syrup recipes you need for the drinks in this book.

MAKES 1 CUP
simple syrup (1:1)

1 cup sugar

◆

1 cup water

Heat the sugar and water in a saucepan over medium heat, stirring occasionally, until the sugar has dissolved. Remove from the heat, let cool, and then refrigerate. Stored in a tightly sealed container, the syrup keeps for a week.

MAKES ½ CUP
Rich simple syrup (2:1)

1 cup sugar

◆

½ cup water

Heat the sugar and water in a saucepan over medium heat, stirring occasionally, until the sugar has dissolved. Remove from the heat, let cool, and then refrigerate. Stored in a tightly sealed container, the syrup keeps for a week.

Honey Syrup (1:1)

1 cup honey

◆

1 cup water

Heat the honey and water in a saucepan over medium heat, stirring occasionally, until the ingredients have integrated. Remove from the heat, let cool, and then refrigerate. Stored in a tightly sealed container, the syrup keeps for a week.

Rich Honey Syrup (3:1)

1 cup honey

◆

⅓ cup water

Heat the honey and water in a saucepan over medium heat, stirring occasionally, until the ingredients have integrated. Remove from the heat, let cool, and then refrigerate. Stored in a tightly sealed container, the syrup keeps for a week.

Grenadine

2 cups POM pomegranate juice

◆

1 cup sugar

◆

2 dashes orange flower water

Combine the juice and sugar in a saucepan and place over medium-high heat. Stir frequently and bring to just under a boil. Reduce the heat to just under a simmer and cook for 20 to 30 minutes. When the syrup has darkened and is thick enough to coat the back of a metal spoon, it's ready. Remove from the heat and let cool. Add the orange blossom water and stir. Label, date, and refrigerate. It keeps for 4 weeks.

Old-Fashioned Cocktails

By the reasoning of this book, the term "Old-Fashioned cocktail" means drinks that adhere to the original definition of a cocktail as a simple libation that includes spirit, sugar, and bitters. And, yes, that definition does include *the* Old-Fashioned.

THE OLD-FASHIONED

If I had wanted to, I could have filled out the recipe portion of this book solely with spins on the Old-Fashioned. The original Old-Fashioned—spirits, bitters, and sugar—is the three-ingredient granddaddy of the cocktail world. And since bartenders rediscovered the true nature of the drink in the early years of this century (that is, sans seltzer, soda pop, or extraneous fruit), they have been churning out variations on the theme on a daily basis until there are now as many three-ingredient Old-Fashioned twists as there are postal codes. More, probably.

I covered a good many of these new drinks in my 2014 book, *The Old-Fashioned: The World's First Classic Cocktail, with Recipes and Lore*. Here I include a few more.

The Old-Fashioned began its long and tangled journey through American bars as the Whiskey Cocktail, an early-nineteenth-century mix of whiskey, bitters, and sugar that was served in a footed wine glass and often downed as a morning drink. The drink picked up in popularity as the century crawled on. It acquired its current name sometime in the late 1800s, as drinkers, alarmed by all the new-fangled add-ons barkeeps were throwing into drinks (such as maraschino liqueur, absinthe, Curaçao, and Chartreuse), began to ask for an "Old-Fashioned Whiskey Cocktail." "Old-Fashioned" became the shorthand term for the drink over time.

The cocktail survived Prohibition but emerged at the other end in a fruitier fashion. A muddled orange slice and cherry, topped with whiskey, bitters, and sometimes soda water, became the common bar treatment and preferred patron style. That construct held for a good long time until modern mixologists brought the drink back to its "garbage-free," pre-Prohibition model. The new-old Old-Fashioned was all about simplicity: delicious whiskey, beautiful ice (often a single large cube), and an orange or lemon twist—a cocktail as imagined by abstract expressionist Mark Rothko: solid, simple, significant.

The world has gone even more Old-Fashioned crazy since my book was published. The inimitable flavor combination has leapt out of the glass and been applied to candles, cheeses, candies, beer, and desserts. It's flattering to the old drink, I'm sure, that it has inspired such imitation, but also a bit undignified and diluting. When you've reached a place where cocktail menus have an Old-Fashioned section, with several selections, you're getting very close to the place where the Martini and its many derivative "'tinis" tumbled into the abyss back in the 1990s.

Thankfully, of all the different versions out there, the classic whiskey one is the standard that prevails in popularity by a wide margin. (I've included a couple worthy post-2012 riffs here as well, for good measure.)

Ogden Nash, a singular unspooler of clever light verse, is well known for a few lines he dashed off in tribute to the Martini—the bit that begins, "There is something about a Martini, a tingle, remarkably pleasant. . . ." If it's been quoted once, it's been quoted ten thousand times. Few know, however, that this was just the first stanza of a longer poem—apparently written on commission as promotional material for the Continental Distilling Corporation—in which many mixed drinks were paid tribute, including the Old-Fashioned. As the rhyme somehow escaped me while researching *The Old-Fashioned*, I am including it here. We shall forgive Nash the bit about the pineapple slice.

> There is something about an old-fashioned
> That kindles a cardiac glow;
> It is soothing and soft and impassioned
> As a lyric by Swinburne or Poe.
> There is something about an old-fashioned
> When dusk has enveloped the sky,
> And it may be the ice,
> Or the pineapple slice,
> But I strongly suspect it's the rye.

Old-Fashioned whiskey cocktail

This is the basic formula for an Old-Fashioned, be it 1887 or 2017. Whether you reach for mellow bourbon or spicy rye is a matter of choice; both work wonderfully in the drink. If you're lacking a muddler (or gumption), a bar spoon of simple syrup will do the job of the sugar cube.

2 ounces bourbon or rye

2 dashes Angostura bitters

1 sugar cube

Orange twist

Saturate a sugar cube with bitters and a bar spoon of warm water at the bottom of an Old-Fashioned glass. Muddle until the sugar dissolves. Add whiskey and stir. Add one large piece of ice and stir until chilled, about 30 seconds. Twist a piece of orange zest over the drink and drop into the glass.

TOBY CECCHINI, 2014

Trinidad Old-Fashioned

It takes a little bit of searching to find the ingredients for this simple but excellent drink. You can order the cider syrup from Wood's Cider Mill in Vermont. The other two products you can find in the better boutique liquor stores.

2 ounces Plantation Trinidad Old Reserve rum

1 scant bar spoon Wood's Boiled Cider Syrup

2 to 3 dashes St. Elizabeth's Allspice Dram

Lemon twist

Orange twist

Stir all the ingredients, except the lemon and orange twists, together over ice in a mixing glass and strain into a large rocks glass or Double Old-Fashioned glass filled with one large ice cube. Twist a piece of lemon zest and a piece of orange zest over the drink and drop into the glass.

ROBERT SIMONSON

Eau Claire Old-Fashioned

Ask for an Old-Fashioned in Wisconsin and you get a drink made with domestic brandy poured over the muddled pulp of sugar, an orange slice, and a maraschino cherry, and topped with soda pop (as soft drinks are still called in the state) or soda water. This drink is a refined version of the same, with cognac stepping in for the local brandy, and the fruit mimicked by the cherry bitters and orange twist—a Wisconsin Brandy Old-Fashioned in a tuxedo, if you will. If you can't find the Ferrand, substitute an equally dry quality brand. (Bittercube is, appropriately, a Wisconsin brand, but available nationwide.) The drink is named after Eau Claire, a mid-sized city in upper Wisconsin founded by French explorers, who would have known their cognac.

2 ounces
Pierre Ferrand
1840 cognac

◆

1 bar spoon
simple syrup (1:1)
(page 10)

◆

3 dashes
Bittercube
Cherry Bark
Vanilla bitters

Orange twist

Combine the syrup and bitters in an Old-Fashioned glass. Add the cognac and stir. Add one large ice cube and stir until chilled, about 30 seconds. Twist a piece of orange zest over the drink and drop into the glass.

Improved cocktails

"Improved cocktails" is a phrase coined in the mid-nineteenth century that has been resurrected in recent years by drink historians. It's a fairly vague term meaning any old-style cocktail to which an enhancement or bit of flair has been applied, be it a dash of this or that ingredient or a twist of lemon. It is used exceedingly loosely in this section to bring together drinks—both classic and modern— that go beyond the old spirit-sugar-bitters model, including a great many of the mighty vermouth-based classics that emerged from the 1880s on.

MARTINI

That cocktail silhouette that you see flashing on and off outside older bars? That's a Martini glass. Nobody has to say it. Everyone knows. What other drink, after all, is so iconic it would get the neon treatment?

The Martini is the undisputed monarch of cocktails. Its reign has been longer than that of Queen Elizabeth II. The frosty, austere, all-alcohol icon has bewitched palates and imaginations for more than a century, to a measure no other drink can even approach. Journalist H. L. Mencken called it "the only American invention as perfect as the sonnet." Author Bernard DeVoto wrote it was "the supreme American gift to world culture." These men said these things with a straight face.

There were other royals before it. The Mint Julep, Sherry Cobbler, Tom Collins, and more—all had their moments on the throne. But none has ruled as long as the Martini. It's the rock and roll of cocktails; once it gripped the charts in the mid-1950s, no other form of music stood a chance. The contest was over.

The drink we all think of when we think of a Martini—still, after all this time—is the super-dry, bracingly strong, ice-cold glass of gin that became popular during the decades following World War II among the men in gray flannel suits who were simultaneously basking in America's economic and cultural zenith and fighting off postwar blues. That particular Martini was served in triplicate at business lunches, was festooned with as many olives as you could jam on a toothpick, and enjoyed only a passing acquaintance with vermouth. It snubbed bitters outright. It was a strong drink drunk by strong personalities.

It was not always thus. And, thank heaven, it is not thus today. Mixologists, armed with out-of-print cocktail manuals they had no intention of returning to the library, brought the vermouth back to pre-Prohibition proportions and, once they could find the stuff, spiced up the mix with a few dashes of orange bitters.

This brought the drink closer to its original profile and made it, strictly speaking, a true "cocktail" again (that is, a drink with bitters somewhere in the equation).

That said, this restoration was, in truth, a bit of a whitewashing of the Martini's history, which is about as complicated as they come. For a drink with such a ramrod reputation for not messing about, the Martini was a troubled child, a real head case that took a while figuring out just what it wanted to be when it grew up. In early recipes, from the late 1800s, the ratios between gin and vermouth were all over the place. And early on, the gin in question was the sweeter Old Tom, not the juniper desert of London dry. The vermouth, meanwhile, was the sweet sort as often as it was dry. It took years before we got to what we now recognize as the Martini, the dry Martini, with no sweetness about the vermouth or the gin.

The Martini settled down and straightened its tie by the 1930s. That was around the time when men started making quasi-poetic, quasi-fascistic statements about it and began challenging each other to swizzle sticks at ten paces when they disagreed as to proportions or whatnot.

That Martini mind-set persists to this day. When someone orders a Martini in a bar, you can bet he or she has a recipe in mind. It's like steak. People know how they want it.

Martini

Like everybody else, I have my own ideas of what makes a great Martini. Three to one suits me, proportion-wise. It hits the sweet spot between dry and wet. I like a number of gins for this recipe, depending on my mood: Beefeater if I want a more assertive drink; Plymouth if I want a more elegant one; Bombay (not Sapphire) if I want something down the middle. If you can find the higher-proof Gordon's that is available overseas and in Duty Free shops, that makes a good, traditional drink, too. Dolin dry vermouth is a good choice for all. For a garnish, the lemon twist is the natural choice to me, as it marries well with the botanical components of many London dry gins. I prefer my olives on the side in a little dish, next to the nuts.

2¼ ounces gin

¾ ounce dry vermouth

1 dash orange bitters

Lemon twist

Combine all the ingredients except the lemon twist in a mixing glass filled with ice and stir until chilled, about 30 seconds. Strain into a chilled coupe. Express a lemon twist over the drink and drop into the glass.

obituary cocktail

Basically, this is a Martini made exotic by a splash of absinthe. If this ends up being your deathbed drink, you didn't do too badly.

2 ounces gin

¼ ounce dry vermouth

¼ ounce absinthe

Lemon twist

Combine all the ingredients except the lemon twist in a mixing glass filled with ice and stir until chilled, about 30 seconds. Strain into a chilled coupe. Express a lemon twist over the drink and drop into the glass.

IAN FLEMING

vesper

Ian Fleming and his famous creation, James Bond, taught a couple of generations how to order Martinis badly, with that "shaken, not stirred" nonsense. But they also gave the world this drink, which first appeared in the 1953 novel *Casino Royale*.

3 ounces gin

1 ounce vodka

½ ounce Lillet Blanc

Lemon twist

Combine all the ingredients except the lemon twist in a mixing glass filled with ice and stir until chilled, about 30 seconds. Strain into a chilled coupe. Express a lemon twist over the drink and drop into the glass.

Japanese Cocktail

One of the oldest and most perfect of three-ingredient cocktails, and a drink widely respected among bartenders, the Japanese Cocktail first saw print in 1862 but remains stubbornly unknown and underappreciated. Perhaps it is too intimidating to be truly beloved. The combination of strong brandy and thick, rich orgeat can knock you on your heels at first sip if you're unfamiliar with it—hell, even if you are familiar with it. It is the ultimate nightcap. It is also a rare cocktail that was actually invented by that paragon of mid-nineteenth-century mixology, Jerry Thomas. If this drink alone had been his legacy, it would be enough for us to honor his name.

2 ounces cognac

◆

½ ounce orgeat

◆

2 dashes
Angostura
bitters

Combine all the ingredients in a mixing glass filled with ice and stir until chilled, about 30 seconds. Strain into a chilled coupe. Express a lemon twist over the drink and drop into the glass.

Lemon twist

ADA CALHOUN

Hanky Panky

One of the best drinks to come out of the legendary American Bar in London's Savoy Hotel is a fine early use of Fernet Branca. The two dashes go a long way.

1½ ounces gin

1½ ounces sweet vermouth

2 dashes Fernet Branca

Orange peel

Combine all the ingredients except the orange peel in a mixing glass filled with ice and stir until chilled, about 30 seconds. Strain into a chilled coupe. Express an orange twist over the drink and drop into the glass.

Alaska

This is one of the oldest and best cocktail applications of yellow Chartreuse. I here advocate an early recipe that calls for Old Tom gin found in Jacques Straub's 1914 work *Drinks*. I find it results in a wonderfully elegant and mellow drink. More commonly, recipes for the Alaska call for London dry gin, which also works well enough.

**2 ounces
Old Tom gin**

**1 ounce yellow
Chartreuse**

**2 dashes
orange bitters**

Combine all the ingredients in a mixing glass filled with ice and stir until chilled, about 30 seconds. Strain into a chilled coupe.

Kangaroo

Martini purists would have been saved so much aggravation over the last half-century if lovers of vodka Martinis had just stuck to one of the drink's original names, Kangaroo, rather than co-opt the hallowed Martini name. Recipes for the Kangaroo omit bitters, which were more common to the recipes named "Vodka Martini." But I'd rather promulgate this name so we can all live in peace.

2¼ ounces vodka

¾ ounce dry vermouth

2 dashes orange bitters

Lemon twist

Combine all the ingredients except the lemon twist in a mixing glass filled with ice and stir until chilled, about 30 seconds. Strain into a chilled coupe. Express a lemon twist over the drink and drop into the glass.

GIBSON

In the annals of mixed drinks, the Gibson is a kind of spectral presence. Though more than a century old, and enshrined in classic films like *North by Northwest* and *All About Eve* (always a good way to enter the cocktail canon), the drink still ranks as an also-ran, shivering in the massive shadow cast by its larger-than-life cousin, the mighty Martini.

Bartenders sense the drink's self-esteem issues and aren't always sure how to address them. If you ever want to cast mixologists into a quandary, ask them whether they consider the Gibson a cocktail in its own right or merely a Martini with an onion. They will pause, looking thoughtful, even troubled, for a fleeting moment, before carefully delivering their answer. No two replies will be the same.

Essentially, a Gibson is a mixture of London dry gin and dry vermouth, with a pickled cocktail onion serving as the garnish. Part of the reason why the Gibson was, for a while, such a laggard in the cocktail revival may be that garnish. Mixology mavens have routinely made their own cherries and bitters for some time now. The cocktail onion, however, doesn't seem to have been worth the trouble. Even today, when you order a Gibson at many respected drinking dens, the bartender will often fish two or three flavorless white orbs from a slim jar bought at D'Agostino. This is wrong. Tiny, store-bought onions bring no more to the drink, flavorwise, than the toothpick that binds them together. If the onion is what makes a Gibson a Gibson, it ought to be fussed over and perfected.

Lately, though, the long-suffering drink has been getting some much-needed love. A handful of prominent cocktail bars in New York, San Francisco, and elsewhere are doing the Gibson up proud. The new breed of Gibson standard-bearers all pickle their own plus-size alliums, each with a very personal twist. The big boys now on parade subtly perfume the gin and vermouth. They contribute. They also make for a great finale, a savory snack at drink's end that's equally as good as the liquid that precedes it.

Ryan Fitzgerald, an owner at the bar ABV in San Francisco, which serves a superlative Gibson, thinks the drink may be its own side dish. "It's so nice to have a bite of that pickled onion, then sip some more, then have another bite," he said. "The Gibson's almost more a food pairing than it is a Martini."

By the standards invoked in this book, the Gibson is technically a two-ingredient drink, as it historically doesn't call for bitters, and we are not counting garnishes in our ingredient tally. But, happily, some of the nouveau Gibsons being served today add sweeter blanc vermouth to the mix (instead of, or in addition to, straight dry vermouth), as well as a bit of onion brine. This nudges the drink into three-ingredient territory.

The recipe featured here belongs to Meaghan Dorman of Dear Irving, which may serve the best Gibson in New York City. Dorman uses only Carpano Bianco vermouth—no dry vermouth at all—making for a much sweeter, smoother Gibson, along with some brine. It's an unusual take, but a harmonious one.

As to the drink's identity crisis, the deciding factor, according to Dorman, may not be the onion at all, but the drink's tenacious nomenclature. The name "Gibson" was first applied to a gin-vermouth mixture in the late 1890s in San Francisco. If the drink were such a weak pretender to the Martini throne, the title Gibson should have died out decades ago. But it hasn't.

That seals the deal as far as Dorman is concerned. "People don't give you the option of 'Martini with twist, olive, or onion,'" she said. "It's always, 'twist or olive?' That makes the Gibson a separate thing."

Meaghan Dorman's Gibson

Dorman's version of the Gibson has become the signature drink of her Gramercy Park bar, Dear Irving. The recipe she uses for cocktail onions comes from Todd Thrasher, the king of cocktails down in Alexandria and Arlington, Virginia.

**2 ounces
Tanqueray 10**

**1 ounce
Carpano Bianco
vermouth**

**¼ ounce onion
brine (page 42)**

**Cocktail onion
(page 42)**

Combine all the ingredients except the cocktail onion in a mixing glass filled with ice and stir until chilled, about 30 seconds. Strain into a chilled coupe. Garnish with the cocktail onion.

cocktail onions

This recipe for homemade cocktail onions is a lot simpler than it first looks. Invest the time. It's worth it. "Pickling spice" can be found in most supermarkets among the other spices.

4 cups distilled champagne vinegar

◆

3 cups warm filtered water

◆

2 cups white sugar

◆

2 tablespoons kosher salt

◆

1 tablespoon pickling spice

◆

1 pound pearl onions, peeled

In a saucepan, combine the champagne vinegar, filtered water, sugar, and salt, and mix until completely dissolved. Set aside.

Pour the pickling spice into a sachet of cheesecloth and place in the vinegar mixture. Add the onions to the vinegar mixture, making sure they are completely covered with liquid, and bring to a boil for only 1 minute (it's important to limit the boil; otherwise, they will lose their crunchy texture).

Remove from the heat and separate the onions from the brine until the brine cools to room temperature, about 15 minutes. Transfer the onions and liquid to a clean glass jar and refrigerate. Cocktail onions can be kept refrigerated for up to 2 months. Once they start to turn dark, it's time to make a new batch.

chrysanthemum

The Chrysanthemum is a fair flower indeed. This is a rare drink in which that typical supporting player, dry vermouth, plays a starring role. Massively underrated, the Chrysanthemum is perfect at the beginning of an evening. But I've also had it at the end of the night and been quite content.

2 ounces dry vermouth

1 ounce Benedictine

3 dashes absinthe

Orange twist

Combine all the ingredients except the orange twist with ice in a mixing glass and stir until chilled, about 30 seconds. Strain into a chilled coupe. Twist a piece of orange zest over the drink and drop into the glass.

MANHATTAN

There have been only a handful of seismic shifts in the evolution of the cocktail. But the arrival of vermouth on the American scene in the late nineteenth century is surely one of them. The cocktail canon would be significantly poorer without this oft-maligned miracle ingredient. The Martini, the Manhattan, the Rob Roy, the Negroni, the Star, the Gibson, the Bronx—they all need vermouth. The list goes on and on. The fine qualities that vermouth brings to these cocktails are difficult to overstate. But then again, vermouth didn't do badly by the arrangement, either. The relationship was symbiotic, and there was ladder climbing on both sides. There's a well-known quote about what the twentieth century's most famous dancing duo, Fred Astaire and Ginger Rogers, did for one another: "He gives her class and she gives him sex. That applies here to the Manhattan as well. Vermouth gave whiskey class, and whiskey gave vermouth sex.

Martini drinkers may not want to read this next part. Historically speaking, their usual is nothing more than the Manhattan's little brother. That unknown American genius who first decided to combine a spirit with sweet vermouth did so with whiskey—because, don't we always try things out first with whiskey? The Martini came shortly afterward.

Like the Martini, the Manhattan went through some growing pains before it gelled into the bourbon/rye-sweet vermouth-bitters concoction we all know and love. Once there, it showed itself to be a solid, secure, and sophisticated drink, a cocktail built like a brick house. And it has ever after attracted a very solid, secure, and sophisticated kind of drinker. Manhattan drinkers know who they are and what they like. (John Pierpont "J. P." Morgan, the enduring and terrifying model for all titans of industry to follow, ordered one at the end of every trading day.) They're so confident in their choice, in fact, that they fret not at all about ordering a drink that has an actual cherry in it—a bright red garnish that is as odd as an olive when it comes down to it, and brushes the border of just plain silliness

More than most of the classic cocktails, the Manhattan's history has been fairly steady. It didn't wake up after Prohibition having shed its bitters or having left its vermouth in its other coat or suddenly having signed for an unordered shipment of extra fruit. It was still just a Manhattan. And any bar could make you a decent one.

The mixology brigade of the twenty-first century reintroduced the drink to the younger generation in fighting form, using good whiskey—often rye, newly rescued from the dustbins of history—and fresh vermouth and actual cherries. Thus spruced up, the drink returned the favor with unprecedented generosity, offering up its hearty formula as inspiration for countless new variations: the Greenpoint (made with the addition of yellow Chartreuse), the Red Hook (maraschino liqueur, page 48), the Little Italy (Cynar, page 51), the Carroll Gardens (Amaro Nardini), the Cobble Hill (Amaro Montenegro and some cucumber), and the Bensonhurst (dry vermouth, maraschino liqueur, and Cynar). (The "neighborhood drinks," they were called.)

One more thing about the Manhattan. The cocktail's lengthy winning streak can possibly be credited to one secret weapon of which almost no other cocktail can boast: you don't need great whiskey to make a great Manhattan. Celebrated literary imbiber Lucius Beebe once wrote, "It has often been remarked that the most exciting Manhattan is one compounded with ordinary quality bar whiskey rather than the rarest overproof article. It is perhaps the only mixed drink where this generality obtains."

It's true and a great and wonderful mystery. The highfalutin bartenders who reach for high-octane, rare, or expensive whiskey to make the "world's greatest" Manhattan are misguided. The best Manhattans I've had have been made with ordinary and easy-to-acquire bourbon or rye. This makes total sense, given the drink's name, which is taken, after all, from one of the world's great cradles of democracy and equal opportunity.

Manhattan

For this drink, rye is the preferred spirit among most mixologists and the younger set. Its rough edges lend the cocktail added structure. But bourbon has a case to plead. Some choose to split the base spirit between bourbon and rye, and there's something there, too. And then there's the matter of which brand of vermouth to pair the whiskey with. A home bartender can have a lot of fun within this simple formula. Experiment. Your ideal is out there somewhere.

2 ounces bourbon or rye

◆

1 ounce sweet vermouth

◆

2 dashes Angostura bitters

Combine all the ingredients except the brandied cherry in a mixing glass filled with ice and stir until chilled, about 30 seconds. Strain into a chilled coupe. Garnish with the brandied cherry.

Brandied cherry

VINCENZO ERRICO, 2003

Red Hook

The Manhattan/Brooklyn cocktail riff that birthed a dozen others, the Red Hook was first served at the original Milk & Honey, the influential, vest-pocket-sized, speakeasy-style cocktail bar that opened in New York in 1999. This cocktail inspired many other bartenders to toy around with the Manhattan template.

2 ounces rye

½ ounce maraschino liqueur

½ ounce Punt y Mes

Combine all the ingredients in a mixing glass filled with ice and stir until chilled, about 30 seconds. Strain into a chilled coupe.

Star

Here's an apple brandy version of the Manhattan that is nearly as old as its model and just as good. Many vermouth cocktails drifted from equal measures of spirit and vermouth to a 2:1 ratio over the years, usually for the better. This one, however, still benefits from the split-base model, which gives you the full flavor of each ingredient. Some people use Peychaud's bitters in this.

1½ ounces apple brandy

1½ ounces sweet vermouth

2 dashes Angostura bitters

Combine all the ingredients except the lemon twist in a mixing glass filled with ice and stir until chilled, about 30 seconds. Strain into a chilled coupe. Express a lemon twist over the drink and drop into the glass.

Lemon twist

AUDREY SAUNDERS, 2005

Little Italy

This is Audrey Saunders' amaro-inflected spin on a Manhattan. It made its debut at her New York bar, Pegu Club, and quickly established itself as a modern classic. Today, you can find it served at bars far from Mulberry Street.

2 ounces Rittenhouse 100-Proof rye

◆

¾ ounce Martini & Rossi Rosso vermouth

◆

½ ounce Cynar

Brandied cherry

Combine all the ingredients except the brandied cherry in a mixing glass filled with ice and stir until chilled, about 30 seconds. Strain into a chilled coupe. Garnish with the brandied cherry.

Palmetto

Rum Manhattans are not rare beasts. They are served up regularly in tiki bars, and, if you're talking to a rum-head, they may be the only kind of Manhattan he or she drinks. This version dates from the early twentieth century. It called for "St. Croix rum." I recommend Cruzan Estate Diamond or Single Barrel as a modern equivalent. As to the name, it doesn't get as much traction as Rob Roy or Star. If you just want to tell the bartender "Rum Manhattan," go right ahead. But that's one extra syllable between you and your drink.

1½ ounces
Cruzan Single
Barrel rum

◆

1½ ounces
sweet vermouth

◆

1 dash orange
bitters

Combine all the ingredients in a mixing glass filled with ice and stir until chilled, about 30 seconds. Strain into a chilled coupe.

ROB ROY

The Rob Roy is always walking a few paces behind the Manhattan, and the latter gave up a long time ago wondering why it couldn't shake this copycat. "The guy must have something going on to have lasted this long," the shrugging Manhattan said with grudging respect.

The Rob Roy will never get the respect a Manhattan does. Nobody describes a Manhattan as "like a Rob Roy, only with bourbon or rye." It's the other way around. Ol' Rob's the one who pulled the spirit switcheroo and got away with calling itself something else. But the drink's a stubborn, tenacious mixture, and there are still plenty of people who prefer it to its more favored cousin.

Why? They may like blended Scotch a whole hell of a lot. Many people do. Dewar's, Johnnie Walker, Grant's, Famous Grouse, Cutty Sark—these are not no-name brands. They may be contrarians looking for an edge that separates them from the masses. Or they may just be Manhattan drinkers tired of the same-old same-old and looking to mix it up a bit while not taxing their brains too much when settling upon an alternative.

Or—and I strongly suspect this—they are seasoned drinkers who know what's what, and have taken a turn in the evening where they find themselves thirsting for something a bit more potent. Orders for a Rob Roy, I've noticed, tend to come later in the evening, once people are half in the bag. It's all folly, of course. The ABV (alcohol by volume) on your average blended Scotch is roughly the same as your average bourbon or rye. But there's something about the kick of the Scotch that makes the drink feel stronger going down.

I like Rob Roys. They have given me Dutch courage to make bold moves when other cocktails have failed me. And they have played a role in some of the most memorable occasions of my life. In 2012, I gathered a bunch of friends and colleagues together for a farewell dinner at Bill's Gay Nineties, a priceless former speakeasy in midtown Manhattan that was being tossed out by a short-sighted, speculative landlord. At night's end, it was rounds of Rob Roys that were called for as nightcaps. Bill's had no trouble with the order. Rob Roys have a friend in old bartenders. No one has to remind them how they're made.

Rob Roy

There's little benefit in reaching for a top-shelf blended Scotch for a Rob Roy. The serviceable mid-range bottlings will do just fine. Famous Grouse is a good and affordable choice. As for garnish, a cherry is as acceptable here as it is in a Manhattan, but I prefer a lemon twist.

2 ounces blended Scotch

1 ounce sweet vermouth

2 dashes Angostura bitters

Combine all the ingredients except the lemon twist in a mixing glass filled with ice and stir until chilled, about 30 seconds. Strain into a chilled coupe. Express a lemon twist over the drink and drop into the glass.

Lemon twist

Nick Strangeway's Rob Roy

The most memorable Rob Roy I've ever had was devised and prepared by Nick Strangeway, a leading light in the early years of the London cocktail revival, at Hawksmoor Spitalsfield, a restaurant where he was, at the time, in charge of the bar. He used Oak Cross, a modern blended Scotch of great quality made by Compass Box, and Noilly Prat's Ambre vermouth, at that time an obscure product that could only be purchased at the French vermouth company's distillery. (It has since been released commercially.) The combination makes for a wonderfully deep, smooth Rob Roy. Nick, when asked about the drink a decade later, could not recall the exact recipe. But these specifications match my taste memory of the cocktail.

2 ounces Compass Box Oak Cross Scotch

1 ounce Noilly Prat Ambre vermouth

2 dashes Angostura bitters

Lemon twist

Combine all the ingredients except the lemon twist in a mixing glass filled with ice and stir until chilled, about 30 seconds. Strain into a chilled coupe. Express a lemon twist over the drink and drop into the glass.

Bobby Burns

Not too far removed from the Rob Roy, the Bobby Burns is another Manhattan variation named for a famous Scottish figure. The Benedictine is the big difference, adding a warming holiday spiciness to the drink. Ratios vary widely from recipe to recipe. Some suggest adding a bit of Drambuie–as if the drink weren't Scottish enough as it is.

2 ounces blended Scotch

¾ ounce sweet vermouth

½ ounce Benedictine

Lemon twist

Combine all the ingredients in a mixing glass filled with ice and stir until chilled, about 30 seconds. Strain into a chilled coupe. Express a lemon twist over the drink and drop into the glass.

JON SANTER, 2004

Revolver

This drink was created by San Francisco bartender Jon Santer, partly in response to the arrival on the market of Bulleit bourbon. The theatrical employment of a flamed orange twist made it a much-ordered drink for a time.

**2 ounces
Bulleit bourbon**

◆

**½ ounce
coffee liqueur**

◆

**2 dashes
orange bitters**

Orange twist

Combine all the ingredients except the orange twist in a mixing glass filled with ice and stir until chilled, about 30 seconds. Strain into a chilled coupe. Garnish with a flamed orange twist.

To do a flamed orange twist, cut a piece of orange peel about the size of a silver dollar. Light a match and use it to warm the skin side of the peel. Holding the match a few inches above the drink, quickly squeeze the peel in the direction of the match. The oil from the peel will briefly erupt into flame, showering its essence over the drink's surface.

ROBERT SIMONSON

Fair Harvard

I created this drink in 2016 for a cocktail reception that followed a lecture at the Yale School of Architecture, at the request of that school's dean, architect Deborah Berke. As the speaker was from Harvard, serving Harvard cocktails seemed apropos. However, the reception was held in an all-white gallery, which the school feared might be stained by dark liquors, should a cocktail spill. The classic Harvard, which is made of brandy and sweet vermouth, would not do. So I came up with this "fair" version of a Harvard.

2 ounces Pisco

1 ounce bianco vermouth

3 dashes orange bitters

Lemon twist

Combine all the ingredients except the lemon twist in a mixing glass filled with ice and stir until chilled, about 30 seconds. Strain into a chilled coupe. Express a lemon zest over the drink and drop into the glass.

NEGRONI

If a cocktail had an IQ, the Negroni would be at the top of the class. There's just too much going on in that little red head.

First you have the gin, its flavor informed by several botanicals—there's a lot for your taste buds to learn there. Then there's the sweet vermouth, which has gin bested, cramming even more representatives from the natural world into its liquid soup. Finally, Campari, with its unknown mix of herbs and fruits, has them both beat. It's a botanist's dream, this cocktail. It's no mystery that the drink is a favorite among chefs. They like things they can taste and taste and taste.

Negroni adopters know all this about their drink. They tend to be smarties or foodies and know they look good and sound intelligent ordering one, just in case anyone is watching. The siren-red liquid in their mitts acts as a signal to the world that they have joined the ranks of adult drinkers; they have conquered their fear of the bitter. As San Francisco restaurateur Doug "Bix" Biederbeck—who has served thousands of Negronis at his art deco North Beach landmark Bix—once wrote, "Nothing says 'grown up' like a Negroni."

The Negroni is the most famous cocktail to have come out of Italy, a land of light, aperitif-style drinking habits. It was named after a bibulous, globetrotting, rodeo-riding Florentine count who liked his Americanos strong ("some gin in that, please. . . .")—a crazy origin story that nonetheless seems to be true. The cocktail crept along in limited popularity throughout the twentieth century, adopted in the postwar years by the kind of sophisticated-cum-decadent citizens of the world who might pass through the Apennine Peninsula on a regular basis. Ballet star Rudolph Nureyev drank them. Tennessee Williams had his characters sip them in his novel *The Roman Spring of Mrs. Stone*. And Orson Welles discovered the drink while acting in a film in Italy in late 1947. He famously commended the cocktail, in Erskine Johnson's syndicated column, with the almost-too-perfect quote, "The bitters are excellent for

your liver, the gin is bad for you. They balance each other."
(He surely practiced that line. It's too good.)

Still, the drink was never a headliner in the United States. No classic cocktail has gone through such a sustained failure to launch as the Negroni. Too bitter for the meek, too European in temperament altogether, it sat there, gaining only the smallest of followings, mainly in San Francisco.

It wasn't until the twenty-first century that circumstances conspired to grant the Negroni its place in the sun. The drink contained three things that young bartenders were then embracing: the neglected gin, the misunderstood vermouth, and Italian bitters, in this case Campari. These mixologists put the drink on the rocks, instead of "up," in a Martini glass, lending it more seriousness.

Countless Negroni riffs followed in short order. (A few of the more notable ones are listed in the following pages.) Today, thousands of Negronis are passed over the bar every night. There are barrel-aged Negronis and Negronis on tap. In 2016, Campari released its own bottled Negroni.

It only took a century.

Negroni

I prefer the classic 1:1:1 proportions on a Negroni. If you like a stronger drink (and many do), go for 1½ ounces of gin.

1 ounce London dry gin

1 ounce sweet vermouth

1 ounce Campari

Orange twist

Combine all the ingredients except the orange twist in a rocks glass filled with one large piece of ice. Stir until chilled, about 30 seconds. Express an orange twist over the drink and drop into the glass.

WAYNE COLLINS, 2001

white Negroni

One of the great modern twists on the Negroni model, this drink has shown a lot of staying power since Wayne Collins, a British bartender, invented it on the fly in 2001. Collins, while working in France, was charged with making Negronis but couldn't find any Campari or sweet vermouth, so he used what he could lay his hands on (French products like Lillet and Suze, naturally). This was the result.

1 ounce
Plymouth gin

◆

1 ounce
Lillet Blanc

◆

1 ounce Suze

Grapefruit twist

Combine all the ingredients except the grapefruit twist in a mixing glass filled with ice and stir until chilled, about 30 seconds. Strain into a chilled coupe. Express a grapefruit twist over the drink and drop into the glass.

Cynar Negroni

This Negroni variation asks for the Italian, artichoke-flavored Amaro Cynar instead of Campari. It has flown under various names, with no clear favorite. When I'm drinking one of these, I like it as well as a classic Negroni.

1 ounce
London dry gin

1 ounce sweet
vermouth

1 ounce Cynar

Orange twist

Combine all the ingredients except the orange twist in a rocks glass filled with one large piece of ice. Stir until chilled, about 30 seconds. Express an orange twist over the drink and drop into the glass.

ERSKINE GWYNNE

Boulevardier

Created in the 1920s by a profligate, Paris-dwelling, expatriate scion of the Vanderbilt clan, the Boulevardier is named after the magazine he briefly published there. The recipe first appeared as a footnote in Harry McElhone's *Barflies and Cocktails* published in 1927. It has, over the last decade, become widely served and greatly loved. As with the Negroni, many choose to increase the amount of bourbon.

1 ounce bourbon

1 ounce sweet vermouth

1 ounce Campari

Orange twist

Combine all the ingredients except the orange twist in a rocks glass filled with one large piece of ice. Stir until chilled, about 30 seconds. Express an orange twist over the drink and drop into the glass.

WILLIAM ROBERTSON

old pal

From the same era as the Boulevardier, the Old Pal is made with rye and dry vermouth. This is a sharper drink, as you might expect, but one with its own flinty appeal. Credit for this one goes to journalist William "Sparrow" Robertson. As for the amount of rye, you know the drill.

1 ounce rye

1 ounce dry vermouth

1 ounce Campari

Orange twist

Combine all the ingredients except the orange twist in a rocks glass filled with one large piece of ice. Stir until chilled, about 30 seconds. Express an orange twist over the drink and drop into the glass.

PHIL WARD, 2016

old Gal

This drink was created by Phil Ward, while working at Brooklyn's Long Island Bar, as a sort of rounder answer to the Old Pal. The blanc vermouth, put in place of the usual dry, softens the effect of the rye and Campari.

1½ ounces rye

◆

1 ounce blanc
vermouth

◆

1 ounce
Campari

Orange twist

Combine all the ingredients except the orange twist in a rocks glass filled with one large piece of ice. Stir until chilled, about 30 seconds. Express an orange twist over the drink and drop into the glass.

DAN GREENBAUM, 2012

Remember the Alimony

This is one of the best of the modern sherry cocktails out there. Dan Greenbaum created it in 2012 at the short-lived New York City cocktail bar The Beagle. It continues to be served—but maybe only because I keep ordering it and writing about it.

1¼ ounces fino sherry

1¼ ounces Cynar

¾ ounce Beefeater gin

Orange twist

Combine all the ingredients except the orange twist in a rocks glass filled with one large piece of ice. Stir until chilled, about 30 seconds. Express an orange twist over the drink and drop into the glass.

JACQUES BEZUIDENHAUT, 2005

La Perla

A lovely and unique mixture of unusual suspects, this drink is the work of South Africa–born San Francisco bartender Jacques Bezuidenhaut. Created in 2005, it was ahead of its time in its use of tequila and sherry as base spirits.

1½ ounces reposado tequila

1½ ounces manzanilla sherry

¾ ounce pear liqueur

Lemon twist

Combine all the ingredients except the lemon twist in a mixing glass filled with ice and stir until chilled, about 30 seconds. Strain into a chilled coupe. Express a lemon twist over the drink and drop into the glass.

SOTHER TEAGUE, 2012

Black Rock chiller

This is a stand-out example in the odd modern trend of serving drinks at room temperature. Sother Teague was a pioneer in these drinks, called scaffas, and has long served this cocktail at his bar, Amor y Amargo, in New York's East Village.

¾ ounce
Branca Menta

♦

¾ ounce
reposado
tequila

♦

¾ ounce Suze

Combine all the ingredients in a rocks glass. Stir briefly, without ice, and serve at room temperature.

Sours

Sours are sour because they contain citrus, be it lemon, lime, orange, or grapefruit juice. The category is one of the oldest in mixology and includes some of the best known and best loved and most lasting cocktails in history.

TOM COLLINS

Imagine your name was Tom Collins. It would be a bit like being John Smith, wouldn't it? A pretty dull handle. Not much to it. Not very memorable. You might meet a Tom Collins and forget him instantly. He is, after all, literally just some Tom, Dick, or Harry.

That's sort of how people tend to think of Tom Collins, the cocktail. It's not really a drink people contemplate. It's out there. It exists. But nobody really requests it and thinks they're in for anything particularly special. It's something of an "I give up" sort of order, a choice for a young, inexperienced drinker or an unadventurous bourgeoisie.

In fact, this is exactly what I thought of the drink when, having just turned eighteen—then the legal drinking age in Wisconsin—I ordered one (with the approval of my mother) at the Elm Grove Inn. My drinking experience up to that point was next to nil. Yet I knew, somehow, in the back of my brain, that the Tom Collins would not get me into too much trouble.

This is an unjust fate for a drink that had one of the most lively beginnings in cocktail history. A laugh riot that swept American barrooms in 1874 had that ol' rascal Tom at its center. The hoax would begin with some innocent being asked if he had seen Tom Collins. "Tom Collins who?" the sucker would reply. Why the Tom Collins that has been talking trash about you all over town! Once the dupe was sufficiently lured in and lathered up by these reports of slander, he was furnished with the choice bit of information that said reprobate Collins was just around the corner in the next tavern. The poor sap would then slam his glass down on the bar, hastily pay his tab, and set out in hot pursuit. Thus would begin a wild goose chase, sending him from bar to bar, in search of the elusive Collins.

This, my friends, is how America amused itself in the days before memes and GIFs.

Newspapers soon got in on the joke, posting bogus notices in their pages about how Tom Collins had been seen hopping a train or exiting a hotel or getting up to this or that mischief. Journalists had a healthier sense of humor about the practical applications of their trade back then.

You'd think that a drink that started as a joke would fade away and fade away quick. But the Tom Collins endured. It helped that it had hearty roots leading all the way back to England, where it was called John Collins and came in punch form. It also helped that it tasted great.

For some reason, modern-day writers and drinkers like to diminish this drink. They term it, with barely conceived dismissiveness, nothing more than spiked fizzy lemonade, or some such damning phrase. Maybe this is because the drink is inextricably linked with summer, and people tend to think of summer drinks as simple-minded refreshments. Or maybe it is due to the lowered expect-ations brought on by decades of badly made Tom Collinses, laced with toxic sour mix, or the post-Prohibition proliferation of bottled Tom Collins or collins mixes. It seems as though nary a fresh lemon was manually squeezed in service of this drink for much of the Cold War.

The only excitement visited upon the Tom Collins in the last quarter century was the recent return to shelves of Old Tom gin. Old Tom is the sweeter version of the spirit that was the original base of the drink. This was a very good development. As much as we all love and respect London dry gin, believe me: Old Tom makes a vastly superior Tom Collins. For some reason, London dry, which makes a Martini stand up straight and packs punch into a Gin and Tonic, renders a Tom Collins thin and uninteresting. The mix of juice and sugar and spirit join much more seamlessly with Old Tom. Suddenly, the drink is rich and flavorful. You might even remember it.

Tom Collins

There are now a number of Old Tom gins on the market from which to choose. Hayman's is a fine choice, but many work well. It is worth your while experimenting with the different brands to see the wide range of Tom Collinses available to you.

2 ounces
Old Tom gin

◆

1 ounce simple
syrup (1:1)
(page 10)

◆

¾ ounce
lemon juice

◆

Soda water

Lemon wedge
and brandied
cherry (optional)

Shake the gin, syrup, and juice with ice until chilled, about 15 seconds. Strain into an ice-filled highball and top with soda water, about 1 ounce. If desired, garnish with a lemon wedge and cherry flag.

Gin Fizz

The difference between a fizz and a collins is that a fizz is not served "long" and comes without ice. But, in this case, it's a difference with a distinction. One is a quick fix, the other a drink to linger over. Both have their time and place. Add an egg white to the shaker and you have a Silver Gin Fizz; an egg yolk, and it's a Golden Fizz.

2 ounces gin

◆

1 ounce simple syrup (1:1) (page 10)

◆

¾ ounce lemon juice

Combine all the ingredients except the soda water with ice in a cocktail shaker and shake vigorously until chilled and frothy, about 15 seconds. Strain into a rocks glass. Top with soda water, about 1 ounce.

Soda water

Bee's Knees

This is a Gin Sour made with honey and a drink that's been around since the 1920s—as you might guess from its flapper-lingo name. Never more than a minor player behind the bar, the drink was rediscovered in the current century by modern mixologists, along with the use of honey as a sweetener.

2 ounces gin

¾ ounce lemon juice

½ ounce honey syrup (1:1) (page 11)

Lemon twist

Combine all the ingredients except the lemon twist in a cocktail shaker filled with ice and shake until chilled, about 15 seconds. Strain into a chilled coupe. Express a lemon twist over the drink and drop into the glass.

SASHA PETRASKE

The Business

A slight variation on the Bee's Knees, this drink is from Sasha Petraske, the man behind the legendary modern speakeasy Milk & Honey. (Say "Bee's Knees" fast and you'll see where the name came from.) Petraske, who died in 2015, was devoted to classic cocktails and pared-down liquid constructions. Fittingly, this drink is an exercise in simplicity and precision. Note that the honey syrup is of the extra thickness typical to Petraske bars.

2 ounces gin

◆

1 ounce lime juice

◆

¾ ounce rich honey syrup (3:1) (page 11)

Lemon twist

Combine all the ingredients except the lemon twist in a cocktail shaker filled with ice and shake until chilled, about 15 seconds. Strain into a chilled coupe. Express a lemon twist over the drink and drop into the glass.

SASHA PETRASKE

Cosmonaut

Another succinct Sasha Petraske creation, this is his sly retort to the popularity of the Cosmopolitan, as the name coyly indicates. Indeed, the drink, piquant and slightly fruity, fills much the same purpose, tastewise, as that ubiquitous cocktail—only more so.

2 ounces gin

¾ ounce lemon juice

1 bar spoon raspberry preserves

Combine all the ingredients in a cocktail shaker filled with ice and shake until chilled, about 15 seconds. Strain into a chilled coupe.

WHISKEY SOUR

The Whiskey Sour can't catch a break. It had its heyday back in the late 1800s when people couldn't get enough of it. But that was the last time it was trendy. Since then, it has been one of the last kids to be picked for the team. (Every classic cocktail, however prosaic its status may be today, was the cat's meow once upon a time.)

Even during the cocktail renaissance of the last twenty years, it has enjoyed a Rodney Dangerfield existence at best ("I don't get no respect," etc.). David Wondrich, the most eminent drinks historian of our time, delivered the hapless Whiskey Sour a knock-out punch in the pages of *Esquire* at the turn of the twenty-first century, calling it, "the fried-egg sandwich of American mixology: simple, dull, reliable in a pinch. It's nourishing, all right, but not a drink for cocktail time, that hour of luminous blue when the more decorative and flush sectors of civilization exchange witticisms over icy glasses of invigorating drink. Uh-uh. Then, you want gin, vermouth, or some combination of the two. Or, of course, a Manhattan. Something dressy. This? The cocktail in its undershirt."

Ouch.

I hereby take umbrage, and not just because I consider the egg sandwich one of New York's great culinary triumphs. Why such disdain for a drink that lives in the same neighborhood as the vaunted Daiquiri and wildly popular Margarita? Those two drinks are considered seamless liquid poetry, while the Whiskey Sour, for some reason, is thought of as a glass of whiskey at which some clod has thoughtlessly thrown some lemon and sugar.

Without a doubt, the Whiskey Sour suffered more than most drinks during the cocktail's dark ages, made from coast to coast with rancid and off-putting sour mix, instead of fresh juice. But prepared properly (watch your proportions), with vigor (shake that thing!), love (use good whiskey and fresh citrus), and alacrity (pour and serve immediately), the Whiskey Sour is a lively and ridiculously delicious drink that can't help but bend your lips into a smile.

As to recipes, you can argue until the bartender turns the stools upside down just how strong, sweet, or tart you think a good Whiskey Sour should be. My ideal follows. If you don't have simple syrup, a heaping bar spoon of sugar will do. Shake it hard so that you end up with little splinters of ice on the surface of the drink.

A lot of otherwise sensible bartenders like to garnish this drink with a cherry-orange slice "flag." To me, that's like taking a dog with a perfectly handsome natural coat and dressing it in a Christmas sweater. Let's leave the drink its dignity, shall we?

whiskey sour

This drink doesn't need a top-shelf bourbon, but it does benefit from an above-average and decently aged (more than six years) bourbon. I like Evan Williams Single Barrel or Henry McKenna bonded 10-year-old, both of which have punch and flavor to burn.

2 ounces
bourbon

◆

¾ ounce rich
simple syrup
(2:1) (page 10)

◆

¾ ounce
lemon juice

Combine all the ingredients in a cocktail shaker filled with ice and shake vigorously until chilled, about 15 seconds. Strain into either a short-stemmed wine glass or a rocks glass.

T. J. SIEGEL, 2001

Gold Rush

A Whiskey Sour rendered silky and viscous by the addition of honey syrup, this drink was a mainstay during the early years of New York bar Milk & Honey. It has since become a modern classic, served worldwide. As with the Whiskey Sour, Henry McKenna bonded ten-year-old bourbon is a good choice for this drink.

2 ounces bourbon

◆

¾ ounce lemon juice

◆

¾ ounce rich honey syrup (3:1) (page 11)

Combine all the ingredients in a cocktail shaker filled with ice and shake until chilled, about 15 seconds. Strain into a rocks glass over one large piece of ice.

Brown Derby

Named for the famous Brown Derby restaurant in Los Angeles, the Brown Derby is a reminder that using honey in a cocktail isn't a new idea and that grapefruit juice can be an excellent citrus alternative to lemon and lime.

2 ounces
bourbon

¾ ounce
grapefruit juice

½ ounce honey
syrup (1:1)
(page 11)

Grapefruit twist

Combine all the ingredients except the grapefruit twist in a cocktail shaker filled with ice and shake until chilled, about 15 seconds. Strain into a chilled coupe. Twist a piece of grapefruit zest over the drink and drop into the glass.

Blinker

This drink, first printed in 1934, looks crazy on paper but is a surprisingly potent and refreshing drink. Modern renditions have tried to twist it into the shape of a traditional sour, but its true identity is as a sort of proto-Greyhound highball. Be sure to use a decent, potent rye, the more powerful the better, and a homemade grenadine.

2 ounces rye

3 ounces grapefruit juice

1 ounce grenadine (page 11)

Grapefruit twist

Combine all the ingredients except the grapefruit twist in a cocktail shaker filled with ice and shake until chilled, about 15 seconds. Strain into a chilled coupe. Twist a piece of grapefruit zest over the drink and drop into the glass.

DAIQUIRI

The Daiquiri is a party drink. There's no getting around it. But the people who drink it have shown up for different kinds of parties. The ones who want the frozen version are looking for one sort of good time while the ones who prefer it the classic way, straight up, are looking for another. But, in the end, both drinkers are loose, easy-going types.

The Daiquiri is a cocktail that asks you to stop, take a moment, enjoy life, and rid your mind of disquieting thoughts. It is a massage of a cocktail. A Martini might move you toward decisive action. A Manhattan can brighten your worldview. An Old-Fashioned may cause you to fall into a brown study, thinking deep thoughts. A Daiquiri, however, will relax you. The most momentous idea to occur to a Daiquiri drinker is "Let's order another Daiquiri."

It makes perfect sense, then, that this tropical mix of rum, lime, and sugar would inspire a concept like the "Daiquiri Time Out," which is exactly what you think it is. It also makes sense that it would be the drink that, when nipped at in small measures, or in prelude to an additional Daiquiri, is sometimes called a "snaquiri." The word and concept is usually credited to New York bartender Karin Stanley.) The drink is very snackable. It's easy to have one, and it's easy to have a second. They're like potato chips.

This laid-back perspective, however, is from the drinker's point of view. From where the bartender is sitting, a Daiquiri can inspire night sweats. Though the cocktail is simple, there is little room for error. A Daiquiri can easily be thrown out of balance. The formula is pitiless. Too much (or too little) sugar or lime juice or the wrong rum, and you're sunk. As a barkeep once told me, "There's nowhere to hide."

The history of the Daiquiri is a curious one, in that credit for its creation is often thrown in the direction of not a bartender, journalist, or liquor company but a mining engineer. Jennings Cox was a rotund, bow-tie-sporting American who worked at an iron mine in Santiago de Cuba, around the time of the Spanish

American war. A happy entertainer, he'd serve his guests pitchers of rum, lime, and sugar, naming the compound after the small town in which he mined: Daiquirí.

Cox hung out at a couple of Santiago bars, the Hotel Venus bar, and the San Carlos Club. There, the drink was converted from a pitcher drink to a cocktail, served in a glass with shaved ice. From there the recipe traveled to Havana, where the added steps of shaking and straining turned it into the libation we know today.

Historians have often dismissed the Cox story. You can't blame them. A mining engineer? It sounds improbable. But Jeff "Beachbum" Berry, a cocktail historian who specializes in all libations tropical, thinks there's a lot of credence to the Cox tale. And Berry doesn't muck about when it comes to cocktail history. "I wouldn't call him the creator," said Berry of Cox. "I'd call him the midwife."

Within a couple of decades, a perfect storm of circumstances—Prohibition, thirsty Americans' sudden interest in traveling to Cuba, and the one-man Cuban publicity machine known as Ernest Hemingway—had conspired to make the Daiquiri "the best-known drink in Cuba," in the words of writer Basil Woon, author of the 1928 book *When It's Cocktail Time in Cuba*.

For cocktail Puritans, it is tempting to believe that the Daiquiri's virtue remained unblemished for a good long time, until the louche 1970s threw the poor thing in a blender. But that's not exactly the case. The ideas "frozen" and "Daiquiri" were never quite strangers, and very few years separate the drink's invention and subsequent reinvention as a frothy drink. Those proto-Daiquiris created by that Santiago bartender were served with shaved ice. And the famous Daiquiris Hemingway guzzled by the dozens at Cuba's El Floridita were of the frosty variety, piled up in the glass like so much applesauce. Woon cautioned that the drink "must be drunk frozen or it is not good."

CONTINUED . . .

Today's serious cocktail bartenders tend to head in both directions, depending on the circumstances, and, if they know what they are doing, both versions are delectable.

If you want the frozen variety, you might want to leave it to the pros. But if you want one that Cox might have served, all you need are your two hands and a shaker. Proportions, as has been mentioned, are vital, but, jigger in hand, they can be mastered and refined. Finding the right rum, however, is trickier. A richer, top-shelf aged rum will not necessarily yield you a better Daiquiri. What you want is a quality white rum, one that is clean and light but with enough character and funk to give the drink's heart a beat. Havana Club Anejo three-year-old rum (technically an aged rum, but with a light touch) is a go-to for many bartenders. If you can lay your hands on it, do.

So, good rum and right proportions in hand: you're set. Nowhere to hide. Except inside your drink.

Daiquiri

Many like to switch the proportions of syrup and lime juice, making for a tarter, drier drink. Others like to eighty-six the syrup in favor of a heaping bar spoon of raw sugar. All fine by me.

2 ounces white rum

1 ounce simple syrup (1:1) (page 10)

¾ ounce lime juice

Lime wheel

Combine all the ingredients except the lime wheel in a cocktail shaker filled with ice and shake until chilled, about 15 seconds. Strain into a chilled coupe. Garnish with the lime wheel (a full, thin slice from the center of the fruit), perching it on the rim of the coupe.

Ti' Punch

This too-little-known drink is the French Caribbean's local DIY Daiquiri. It is specifically associated with Martinique. It is easy as pie to put together—like a Daiquiri Erector set—and a great showcase for the grassy flavors of the islands' own Rhum Agricole. Neisson, Clement, and La Favorite are all good brands to reach for. Cane syrup can be bought in many stores. Clement makes a good version.

**2 ounces
Rhum Agricole**

◆

**1 bar spoon
cane syrup**

◆

Lime wedge

In a rocks glass, combine the syrup and a squeeze of the lime wedge. Add the Rhum Agricole, stir, and then add a few ice cubes and stir again.

SIDECAR

"Properly made, this is an excellent cocktail."

So wrote John Iverson, the author of the 1937 book *Liquid Gems*. Looks like a recommendation on the face of it. But so much hangs on that "properly made."

The Sidecar constitutes brandy's biggest claim to cocktail immortality. It's a simple mix of cognac, curaçao, and lemon juice. The drink is accepted by bartenders and cocktail enthusiasts as a classic, even if it doesn't receive anywhere near the heavy rotation among drinkers that other classics do. It's sort of like *The Scarlet Letter* or *The Red Badge of Courage*—classic works, no argument, but who actually reads those books anymore?

The Sidecar is a Jazz Age baby. One of the oft-mentioned top contenders for having invented the cocktail is Harry's New York Bar in Paris. (The matter of the drink's origin is far from resolved.) However, the recipe published by owner Harry McElhone in his wonderful 1927 book *Barflies and Cocktails*—one part each of brandy, lemon juice, and Cointreau—is not what anyone would call a great Sidecar today. Bartenders don't agree on much, Sidecar-wise, but they do come together in declaring that the 1:1:1 spec, when made with current ingredients, is unpalatable. Rather, they tend to up the portion of brandy.

Part of the challenge of perfecting the Sidecar is that it's easy to royally screw up every one of the three components. Make a Manhattan with basic bourbon and run-of-the-mill sweet vermouth, and it's still a pretty good drink. Take a step down in either of the two alcoholic ingredients in the Sidecar and the cocktail tumbles into the basement. It's a drink that knows a diamond from a rhinestone.

Contributing to the Sidecar's current fate as an afterthought classic is that nobody makes this cocktail their calling card. Other classic cocktails benefit from the attentions of dedicated drinkers who make those mixtures their usual—that is to say, their mission. But the Sidecar drinker—where is this unicorn?

Furthermore, you hear of plenty of bars renowned for their Martini or their Irish Coffee. Surely "Best Sidecar in Town" is a claim that's still up for grabs.

One who might be able to make that boast is Joaquín Simó, as good a bartender as New York has to offer and owner of the bar Pouring Ribbons. He is a Sidecar fan.

"With the Sidecar, it's not so much about flavor for me as it is about mouth feel," he said. The orange liqueurs he knew were not sweet enough to balance out the lemon juice. "These do not cancel each other out. They are not equivalent in the way, say, simple syrup and lemon juice cancel each other out." So he adds a bar spoon of rich Demerara syrup (2:1) to the drink, which otherwise contains 2 ounces of Pierre Ferrand 1840 cognac, a ¾ ounce of Pierre Ferrand dry curaçao, and ¾ ounce of lemon juice.

"I don't want the drink to taste thin or watery halfway through," he continued, "so I bump up the sugar to give up a little more fat." He succeeds. His Sidecar is a whole, not a poorly assembled brandy puzzle. It has a roundness, a sort of luxurious texture, and all three elements are balanced. And the Demerara does the trick the ubiquitous sugar rim was always meant to, but never did.

Though that spoon of syrup technically makes his Sidecar a four-ingredient drink, I am including the recipe here nonetheless, alongside a standard Sidecar recipe. It's too good to exclude. Call it an enhanced three-ingredient cocktail.

sidecar

A good cognac is wanted here, VSOP or better. Martell Cordon Blue is a good brand for this drink. Many old-school recipes call for a sugar rim—don't follow those recipes.

1½ ounces
cognac

◆

¾ ounce
Cointreau

◆

¾ ounce
lemon juice

Combine all the ingredients in a cocktail shaker with ice and shake until chilled, about 15 seconds. Strain into a chilled coupe.

Joaquín Simó's sidecar

While Simó has invented many fine modern drinks, he is especially adept at making classics shine. If you find yourself in his New York bar, Pouring Ribbons, try his Manhattan and Daiquiri as well.

2 ounces Pierre Ferrand 1840 cognac

¾ ounce Pierre Ferrand Dry Curaçao

¾ ounce lemon juice

1 bar spoon rich simple syrup (2:1) (page 10)

Combine all the ingredients in a cocktail shaker with ice and shake until chilled, about 15 seconds. Strain into a chilled coupe.

MARGARITA

We live in an age where cocktail writers regularly climb upon their soapboxes and launch into paeans about particular drinks dear to their hearts. But does anyone wax rhapsodic about the Margarita?

I don't think so. The Margarita is easy to like. It's easy to make. And, God knows, it's easy to find. It's been the most popular cocktail in America for what seems like eons. By the time you finish reading this sentence, thousands of people will have ordered a Margarita somewhere. Jimmy Buffett's "Margaritaville" has been on heavy rotation on the radio and in shopping malls and elevators since 1977. (Rum and Coca-Cola may have its Andrews Sisters and Scotch and Soda its Kingston Trio, but no drink boasts an earworm of the strength and deathlessness of "Margaritaville.")

In short, the drink needs no outside help. No writer has to rush to its rescue, composing prose poems of praise, in hopes that someone, *someone* will finally pay attention.

That's quite a triumph for a cocktail made with tequila, a spirit all but unknown in the States until Prohibition. In 1934, American travel writer Emma-Lindsay Squier described tequila in her book *Gringa: An American Woman in Mexico* as "a distilled product that bites at your stomach like a mad dog and then kicks like an evil-tempered mule." That was a fairly typical reaction. But what were dry Americans to do during the 1920s but cast curious looks over the country's shared borders to see what hooch might be available there?

There are about a baker's dozen of competing origin stories surrounding the creation of the Margarita; there always are when the prize in question is an enormously popular and famous drink. Most seem about as credible as the tabloid headlines at the supermarket checkout. Quite possibly, like most simple cocktails, it came about naturally, not through some sudden stroke of genius by one individual. The main thing to keep in mind here is that a true Margarita has Curaçao, and that there was once a category of drinks know as "daisies," which began to appear in the late 1800s. By the rather vague and slippery definition of the genre, daisies are sours that contain a little something extra, sometimes seltzer, sometimes raspberry syrup, and sometimes Curaçao. The word *margarita* is Spanish for "daisy." There aren't too many dots to connect here.

The Margarita is a food cocktail. Cocktail evangelists have been preaching the gospel of food-cocktail pairings for nearly two decades now, trying to break into the wine monopoly and convince people that, yes, mixed drinks make a good accompaniment with dinner. But the Margarita cracked that nut long ago without even trying. Many a meal at a Mexican restaurant or beach/resort community eatery has been washed down with Margaritas.

The arrival of the Tommy's Margarita in the 1990s made a lot of bartenders and barflies wonder if they'd been making and drinking the cocktail wrong all along. Julio Bermejo, the owner of Tommy's Mexican Restaurant in San Francisco, began making his Margaritas without Curaçao, in order to draw attention to the nuanced natural flavors to be found in the quality tequila he was pouring. His intentions were good, and the drink is good as well. But, as the *New York Times* restaurant critic Pete Wells once tweeted when an editor at a food website insisted that the best Margarita is made without Curaçao, "I look forward to trying your tequila sour."

Margarita

As with the Daiquiri, some like to switch the proportions of sweetener (Cointreau, in this case) and lime juice, making for a more tart drink. Those who don't mind a sweeter drink sometimes add a bit of simple syrup. Be sure to use 100 percent agave tequila. A salted rim is entirely a matter of preference; to avoid dogma either way, try a half rim of salt. Freedom of choice is a wonderful thing.

1½ ounces tequila

1 ounce Cointreau

¾ ounce lime juice

Combine all the ingredients in a cocktail shaker filled with ice and shake until chilled, about 15 seconds. Strain into a chilled coupe or a rocks glass filled with ice, either one half rimmed with salt (optional).

JULIO BERMEJO

Tommy's Margarita

The most famous Margarita variation of the twenty-first century, this is simply a Margarita sans the Curaçao and with agave syrup instead of sugar. Julio Bermejo created it to showcase the natural flavors of the many brands of 100 percent agave tequila he carried at his family's San Francisco restaurant, Tommy's Mexican Restaurant. Agave syrup can be found in most grocery stores.

2 ounces reposado tequila

1 ounce lime juice

½ ounce agave syrup

Combine all the ingredients in a cocktail shaker filled with ice and shake until chilled, about 15 seconds. Strain into a chilled coupe or a rocks glass filled with ice, either one half rimmed with salt (optional).

Brandy Fix

Fixes were a style of drink exceedingly popular in the nineteenth century. They are so enjoyable and easy to manage that it's a bit of a mystery that, even in today's historically minded cocktail era, they remain rather obscure and hard to find at bars. (The late Sasha Petraske, of Milk & Honey fame, was a master at the fix.) A fix is basically a sour served on crushed ice and sometimes adorned with an elaborate garnish. I don't really care about the latter aspect. But the former alteration adds significant allure. The recipe here is for brandy, but the formula works with just about any spirit you care to try. Fixes can get more complex than this, but not necessarily any better.

2 ounces cognac

¾ ounce lemon juice

¾ ounce rich simple syrup (2:1) (page 10)

Lemon wedge

Combine all the ingredients in a cocktail shaker and dry shake (no ice) for about 15 seconds. Strain into a double Old-Fashioned glass filled with crushed ice. Garnish with a lemon wedge. Serve with a straw.

CAIPIRINHA

You don't have to dig too deeply into Brazilian drinking habits before you bump into the Caipirinha. Actually, you'll probably run up against it first thing. It's Brazil's national cocktail and is made with the country's most common and popular indigenous spirit: cachaça. Cachaça is a rumlike distillate. Just don't call it "Brazilian rum" in the presence of any cachaça makers or Brazilian patriots unless you want to start an argument. The country lobbied hard to get the American government to recognize the spirit as a distinct product native to Brazil.

The Caipirinha isn't too far removed from its warm-weather drinking buddies, the Margarita, Ti' Punch, and Daiquiri. All share the tropical trinity of sugar, lime juice, and spirit. In the Caipirinha's case, the lime isn't juiced, but remains relatively intact. A half of a lime, cut into wedges, is muddled with sugar at the bottom of a rocks glass and then topped with cachaça and ice. It's a simple drink—as behooves a refreshment that was born in Brazil's rural hinterlands—even if it does require a little elbow grease.

Americans first began to see the Caipirinha pop up at bars in the 1990s, hot off the heels of the mojito craze, another equatorial drink that involves muddling—in the mojito's case, mint.

However, cachaça's fortunes in the States have changed significantly since the dawn of the new century. Before then, most of the cachaça exported from Brazil was of the industrial sort—rough stuff. Lately, a bunch of artisanal brands have begun to export abroad, including cachaças made from pot stills and cachaças aged in barrels made from all sorts of wood.

In this brave new world of wide cachaça choice, the tried and true Caipirinha can be both a boon and a burden to advocates of the spirit. The Caipirinha remains the cocktail most closely associated with cachaça. It gets drinkers in the door, but often they don't venture beyond the vestibule. Despite the valiant efforts of mixologists, cachaça has a very narrow user profile. Few liquors are so tied in the consumers' mind to a single cocktail.

Still, there are worse headaches to have. Tequila and Pisco struggle with the same problem, vis-à-vis the Margarita and Pisco Sour. And, you know what? They'll be fine. Those spirits will be just fine.

Moreover, all those wonderful, artisanal cachaças may be of little use to the Caipirinha. The drink shares something with the Manhattan in that some think the best versions of the drink are made with run-of-the-mill product. This rule of thumb goes, "The worse the cachaça, the better the Caipirinha."

caipirinha

Lime quality can mean a lot with this drink. Look for a ripe lime with good flesh; a dry, juiceless fruit will not do the job. There are many good cachaça brands on the market now. Leblon and Novo Fogo are two.

2 ounces cachaça

2 bar spoons sugar

½ lime, cut into quarters

In a double Old-Fashioned glass, gently muddle the sugar and lime wedges. Add the cachaça and stir until the sugar dissolves. Add ice and stir until chilled, about 30 seconds.

Jackson Cannon's Jack Rose

This is one of the best known of the apple brandy cocktails. The argument as to whether it's shown to best advantage with lemon juice or lime never seems to end. This recipe (and the formula for the grenadine) belong to Jackson Cannon, a Boston bartender who made this drink his calling card at the bar and restaurant Eastern Standard. He did well.

2 ounces Laird's Bonded Applejack

¾ ounce lemon juice

¾ ounce grenadine (page 11)

Combine all the ingredients in a cocktail shaker with ice and shake until chilled, about 15 seconds. Strain into a chilled coupe.

Highballs

This class of mixed drinks is typically simple, composed of two or
(in the case of this book) three ingredients, only one of them usually
being spirit, and served in its eponymous glass, often over ice.
They have a well-deserved reputation for being refreshing.

GIN AND TONIC

Creative was on vacation when this classic got its name. That sometimes happens when it comes to highballs. "This and That" is as good a name as any. And "Gin and Tonic" is as utilitarian as they come.

The name makes sense when you consider the drink's origins. The two ingredients—gin and quinine—were forced into a shotgun marriage by British military in India trying to ward off malaria. Quinine, which is derived from cinchona tree bark, works against malaria just fine but doesn't taste very good by itself. That's where the gin came in (plus some sugar, water, and citrus). Eventually, the Brits just plain liked the drink on its own merits, regardless of its healthful qualities. Commercially produced tonic water pounced upon the drink's popularity by the late 1800s.

The Gin and Tonic remained a British thing until after World War II, when it began to take hold in America, mainly because tonic water finally became widely available. Throughout the Eisenhower years, it was all the rage in the WASP-ish circles along the Atlantic seaboard. By 1954, the drink was so familiar to the public that the *New York Times*, in a profile of actor Art Carney, felt comfortable in characterizing him as the tonic to Jackie Gleason's gin.

It's reputation as a summer drink was established early on and has never really let up. When the white pants come out of the closet, so does the tonic come down from the shelf.

While ubiquitous and widely consumed, the drink got a rather bad name in the late twentieth century. Because it was so easy to make, bartenders made it with ease, too much ease: tonic water out of a soda gun, desiccated lime wedges, and lousy ice. The next century saw more conscientious efforts to build the drink properly, as well as the arrival of better, artisanal tonic waters that weren't as sweet as the mainstream brands and tasted worlds better.

Back to the name. It's called a Gin and Tonic, sure. But that's never been the whole story. It's Gin and Tonic and Lime. Or Gin and Tonic and Lemon, if you like. For those citrus wedges aren't just garnishes. They're part of the whole deal. The drink isn't the drink without them. It's just, well, some gin and some tonic in a glass. It's not a Gin and Tonic.

Talk to the Spanish and they'll tell you that not even a lemon and a lime combined is sufficient garnish. Over the past couple decades, the Iberian Peninsula has made the drink its own in such a way as to make the British seem like pikers. If Americans are all Norman Rockwell about the drink, the Spanish are more like Salvador Dalí. Out with the highball, in with the goblet. They need that roomy goblet to fit in all the fruits and herbs they throw into the glass. The over-the-top garnishes in a Spanish "Gin Tonic," as they call it, wouldn't look out of place on a front door during the holiday season—rosemary, tarragon, mint, lavender, thyme, basil, you name it. As for the liquid, if you've got a gin, they're willing to give it a try. Same with tonic water. And on and on, in endless combinations, each pairing carefully, or at least imaginatively, thought out. (The Germans have recently become similarly mix-'em-match-'em-collect-'em-all in their Gin and Tonic consumption.)

Once indoctrinated into the Spanish way of the G and T, it can be hard to go back to the somewhat stodgy Anglo-American model. A bulbous and beautiful Gin Tonic crowned with a headdress of botanicals does have a certain Carmen Miranda swagger. But the original model, brisk and brittle, tangy and bright, shouldn't be underestimated. And there's something a little backasswards about taking such a simple drink and making it labor-intensive. You can almost imagine a British officer sniffing, "Well, if it takes that much effort to save a man's life . . ."

Gin and Tonic

Many gins function well in this very forgiving drink. Of course, some work better than others. Among classic London drys, I like Beefeater, Tanqueray, Bombay (not Sapphire), and the overproof Gordon's, if you can find it. Among modern gins, Ford's gin, J. Rieger Midwestern dry gin, and Dorothy Parker American gin are good. If you want a savory, Spanish-style G and T, Gin Mare is excellent. For tonics, avoid the mass-market brands like Schweppes and Seagram's. Craft brands like Fever Tree and Q are miles better. Some prefer a lemon wedge in this drink.

1½ ounces London dry gin

2 to 4 ounces tonic water

Lime wedge

Pour the gin into a highball glass. Fill the glass with ice, top with tonic water, and stir briefly. Squeeze the lime wedge over the drink and drop into the glass.

cuba libre

That's fancy talk for Rum and Coke. But, seriously, there is a difference; the addition of the lime juice makes for a huge assist in stiffening the drink's backbone. For rum, go with your tastes, anything from a white rum to a lightly aged one; some dark rums even work. For the Coke, find a bottle of the Mexican variety that contains cane sugar instead of corn syrup.

2 ounces rum

½ lime

4 ounces Mexican Coca-Cola

Lime wheel

Fill a highball glass with ice. Squeeze half a lime over the ice, add the rum, and top with the Coca-Cola. Stir briefly and then garnish with the lime wheel.

Fumata Bianca

This is a soft, yet edgy mixture of sweet, herbal, and smoky that goes down easy, despite the challenging flavors involved.

**1 ounce
Carpano Bianco**

◆

1 ounce Suze

◆

**½ ounce Del
Maguey Vida
mescal**

Combine all the ingredients except the grapefruit twist in a collins glass. Add ice and top with club soda. Express a grapefruit twist over the drink and drop into the glass.

Club soda

◆

Grapefruit twist

DARK 'N' STORMY

Banging away at a typewriter atop his doghouse, Snoopy began many a literary effort with the hackneyed phrase, "It was a dark and stormy night . . ." The joke was that, for all his lofty aspirations and put-on airs, Snoopy's work wasn't terribly inspired. (As one scholar of the comic strip observed, Snoopy's tragedy is that he wakes up every morning just to realize that he is only a dog.)

This drink's a bit like that. The name promises all sorts of drama and excitement, but the reality of the experience is pretty tame and predictable. We all kind of know where dark rum and lime and ginger beer are going to get us, don't we?

But that doesn't mean there isn't good drinking to be had here. The secret to the success of this drink is its rude depth of flavor. You want that rum funky and murky. You want that ginger beer spicy. And just let limes be limes, because that's usually more than enough.

The drink has roots in Bermuda, which is the home of Goslings, the dark rum closely associated with the highball. The company has made a nuisance of itself by enforcing a trademark on the drink's name, an act of corporate aggression that makes the tradition of using Goslings in a Dark 'n' Stormy less fun than it might otherwise be. Drinkers don't like rules; that's why they drink.

If you want to go all in on the Bermuda thing, find Barritt's Stone Ginger Beer, which has been made on the island nearly as long as Goslings rum. (Goslings also makes its own ginger beer.) And if you want to be even more purist about it, omit the lime juice. Bermudans never make the drink with lime; that was an American addition and, I believe, an improvement.

Unsurprisingly for the drink born on an island, it was first associated with the sailing set. It didn't really start to land on many United States cocktail menus until the 1990s. But it's come into its own over the past decade or two. Today, it's drunk by all sorts of landlubbers, in coastal and land-locked states alike.

Dark 'n' Stormy

For rum, start with Goslings and see how you like it. If you'd like to move on, there are other fine dark rums out there. Just watch out for the Cocktail Police. They'll be the ones wearing Bermuda shorts.

2 ounces
dark rum

½ ounce
lime juice

3 ounces
ginger beer

Combine the rum and lime juice in a collins glass filled with ice. Top with ginger beer and stir briefly.

MOSCOW MULE

Most cocktails are unselfish creations. Yes, there is commerce involved. Drinks are, of course, bought and sold every waking day. Still, the majority of mixtures were born out of no motivation more complicated than to deliver pleasure and good cheer to weary men and women.

The Moscow Mule—one of the oldest of the great vodka cocktails—has always had the whiff of entrepreneurship about it, of larger forces putting something over on the guileless public. It is the cocktail as capitalism, the liquid equivalent of a back-room political deal.

The potion was the fruit of three businesspeople trying, in the early 1940s, to unload three different things that nobody wanted. There was John G. Martin, president of Heublein, Inc., who was trying to cajole Americans to drink his strange and obscure Russian product, Smirnoff vodka. He met up with Jack Morgan, owner of the Cock 'n' Bull on the Sunset Strip, who made a ginger beer in which drinkers were equally uninterested. In some versions of the story, there's a third purveyor of unwanted goods—copper mugs—on hand, but this part of the story has been more difficult to confirm. Bing, bang, boom, and a lime or two—the Moscow Mule was born and took off among the Hollywood crowd. By 1946, the drink was already in the Stork Club cocktail book and, two years later, in David Embury's *The Fine Art of Mixing Drinks*.

The Moscow Mule's initial zenith was pretty brief. By the 1970s, like a lot of once-famous cocktails, it had been largely forgotten and was seldom made until some cocktail scholars began digging into the history of the drink in the early years of the twenty-first century. Young buck mixologists didn't pay much mind; they were too busy rediscovering rye and mezcal and other bold-tasting liquids. They couldn't be bothered with a drink made with the ubiquitous spirit they considered antithetical to their efforts

But vodka companies, looking for a historical foothold in the burgeoning cocktail scene, took note. And so the drink's great second coming began, yet another triumph of capitalism. Vodka reps arrived at bars with boxes of custom-made copper mugs and cases of ginger beer. And if the snootier cocktail bars motioned for the reps to move along, there were plenty of other bars that happily signed up. By the 2010s, the drink was everywhere, nearly as popular as the Bloody Mary or mojito. Eventually, some of the better bars gave in, because there was always going to be a customer asking for a vodka cocktail and better to offer one with a little bit of pedigree than not.

More than any other drink in this book, you need the proper vessel here or don't bother. The mug makes this drink. Always has. Without that glistening copper, the cocktail is robbed of all circumstance and excitement.

Moscow Mule

A fancy, top-shelf vodka will not improve this drink; workhorses like Smirnoff and Stoli will do just fine (and, if you go with Smirnoff, you're being historically accurate). A more important factor here is the ginger beer. Try to use a pungent brand with a lot of kick. The drink is called a mule, after all. Fever Tree makes a good version.

2 ounces
vodka

½ ounce
lime juice

4 ounces
ginger beer

Lime wedge

Combine the vodka and lime juice in a copper mug filled with crushed ice, top with ginger beer. Garnish with a lime wedge.

Mamie Taylor

This Scotch-based predecessor of the Moscow Mule appeared in the early years of the twentieth century and was possibly an inspiration. For those who find the Moscow Mule somewhat lacking in character, give this competitor a shot.

2 ounces
blended Scotch

½ ounce
lime juice

4 ounces
ginger beer

Combine the Scotch and lime juice in a collins glass filled with ice. Top with ginger beer and stir briefly.

HARVEY WALLBANGER

The Harvey Wallbanger is the three-ingredient, fluke colossus that conquered the 1970s. Its reign was intentional, and the campaign was premeditated. If you want to know who was behind the plot, just look at the ingredients: one of these things is not like the others. The vodka and orange juice industries were doing just fine as the "Me Decade" dawned. But Galliano—that yellow stuff from Italy in the ridiculously long bottle—didn't have much of a foothold on American backbars. Ads in the 1960s showed outsized bottles of the stuff posed alongside various Roman ruins. It wasn't working.

So George Bednar got to work. Bednar was a savvy marketing wiz employed by McKesson, the 1960s importer that had America's Galliano account. Galliano needed a new story, a new drink, and a new mascot. What if they were all the same thing?

Bednar hooked up with Antone "Duke" Donato, a short, Runyon-esque, career bartender. Duke was born in Brooklyn, the son of Italian immigrants. As a kid, he ran liquor for bootleggers. After serving with valor in World War II, winning several decorations, he opened a bar in Hollywood called the Black Watch. (As to the bar's odd name, Duke credited the Black Watch Regiment with saving his life during the war. Duke was so grateful that, every year, on the anniversary of his salvation, he would don Black Watch tartan pants.) The Black Watch, which lasted about a decade, became a celebrity haunt. Duke served the likes of Kirk Douglas, Peter Lorre, Red Skelton, Charlton Heston, Sammy Davis Jr., Harry Belafonte, and Shelley Winters. He knew Frank Sinatra. He was that kind of bartender.

Duke also ran a bartending school in Hartford, which is probably where Bednar got wind of him. Duke had invented a couple of drinks using Galliano, including a Screwdriver riff he called—what else?—the Duke Screwdriver. (By the account of Antone's grandson, the drink may have been invented at the Black Watch in the 1950s.) For Bednar, that name wouldn't do. How about something snappy, something silly, something memorable? How

You can't come up with a name like that and not create a person to go with it. So Bednar whipped up two, one human and one cartoon. The human Harvey—fictitious, but Bednar wasn't letting on—was a hard-drinking, wall-banging surfer named Harvey from California on whom Antone had first tested the drink in 1952 and who then lent his name to the cocktail.

For the cartoon "Harvey Wallbanger," Bednar tapped an illustrator named Bill Young, who sketched out a sad sack beach bum in sandals whose mug would soon be plastered over posters and T-shirts and what have you. (Young, who received a percentage of every case of Galliano sold, went from driving a Volkswagen to a BMW.)

It was a finely honed, carpet-bombing ad campaign and it worked like a charm. Harvey Wallbangers were served hand over fist in fern bars and clubs. Galliano became the best-selling liqueur in America—quite an accomplishment given how little of the product actually went into the cocktail. There were Harvey Wallbanger parties and Harvey Wallbanger cake mixes. There were "Harvey Wallbanger for President" buttons. Antone did brand work with both Galliano and Smirnoff vodka.

But the Harvey Wallbagner was no Martini or Manhattan. It had legs, but they weren't very long ones, and by the 1980s it was out of vogue. With the turn of the century, and Galliano's decision to return its juice to the original, more complex recipe, a few young mixologists tried to bring it back—along with other lost 1970s cocktails—with middling success.

Though it will likely never again experience the widespread popularity it did in the 1970s, the drink will never be completely forgotten, any more than eight-track tapes or pet rocks. It has, after all, that unforgettable name going for it.

Harvey wallbanger

Choice of vodka doesn't matter much here. Fresh orange juice does.

1½ ounces
vodka

◆

3 ounces
orange juice

◆

½ ounce
Galliano

Orange wheel

Combine the vodka and orange juice in a highball glass filled with ice and stir. Float the Galliano on top and garnish with the orange wheel.

Other cocktails

◇◇◇

MINT JULEP

Not too many years ago, most any cocktail history tome began with the iconic 1806 definition of the cocktail, as "a stimulating liquor, composed of spirits of any kind, sugar, water, and bitters." But recent scholarship has shown us that the Julep, not the cocktail (as then rigidly categorized), can lay claim to being America's first great mixed drink.

The Mint Julep is the not-quite-sole, but staunchest survivor of one of America's oldest drink genres, one that predates the Revolutionary War and, very likely (sorry, Kentucky), the creation of bourbon. Virginians were compounding Julep-like refreshments with brandy as morning eye-openers in the mid-1700s. Actually, once upon a time, any spirit would do. A quarter of a millennium later, we have, of course, long since settled on bourbon as the requisite spirit.

Southern aristocrats no longer own the libation. Everyone drinks Juleps. Still, it's impossible to order a Mint Julep without a certain air of hauteur. You may not be wearing a white suit or sporting a Van Dyke, but you might as well be. The name of the drink itself is a kind of verbal flourish. Mint Julep could be the name of a character in a Tennessee Williams play.

Perhaps it's due to the drink's association with warm climates, but the Mint Julep drinker lives in the moment. He or she sees no reason to rush; good things take a little time, as do good drinks. As H. I. Williams wrote of the drink in his 1943 book *3 Bottle Bar*, a Mint Julep is "the real McCoy only if the ice is very fine, and the gentle stirring is unhurried. Stop all the clocks and let time stand still for julep parties."

The Mint Julep drinker also sees no reason to suffer unnecessarily. Why be hot when you can be cool? Why bear the bite of whiskey when you can smooth it out with sugar, ice, and mint? Why exert yourself in tipping a glass back when a straw is available?

It's a self-indulgent attitude. How apt, then, that the Mint Julep is the signature drink of the Kentucky Derby, one of the more hedonistic events on the athletic calendar: two minutes of competition surrounded by several days of partying. It's the Mardi Gras of sporting events.

The drink can bring out the poetry hidden deep within the heart of even the most hardened characters, among them journalists. Chris McMillan—a New Orleans bartender, and perhaps the most famous Julep builder in the union—recites, when constructing the drink, an entire article written in the 1890s by a Kentucky newspaperman named J. Soule Smith. "The zenith of man's pleasure," runs one section. "He who has not tasted one has lived in vain."

Whereas journalists go soft in the face of a Julep, politicians, it seems, grow foolhardy. While campaigning to be president in 1860, Senator Stephen Douglas once claimed that the Julep—the ownership of which Kentucky and Virginia have fought over for years—was invented in his native Illinois. And he did this while speaking in Virginia . . . to Virginians!

If the Julep can drive a wedge between a politician and a voter, it, too, can build a bridge between lawman and lawbreaker. An 1893 story in the *Brooklyn Eagle* tells of Ned Marshall, a Kentuckian who became a prominent California lawyer. Marshall drank Juleps with the "hardest case in San Diego County" simply because the thief was the only man in the area whose land sprouted wild mint.

But bonding disparate souls is nothing to the Julep. Why, it can save lives. In 1900, a Southern physician insisted a Brooklyn woman administer weak Mint Juleps to her puny newborn, who was suffering through a painful teething. The mother protested. Might the tot not develop a premature taste for liquor, his life forever ruined? Nonsense, insisted the doctor, who pressed his case until the parent acquiesced.

The baby improved.

Mint Julep

The bourbon you use here should be the bourbon you like. Get fresh mint with full leaves. A slightly wilted or brown mint tuft makes for a sad garnish. And be sure to use a silver julep cup. The Mint Julep is a majestic drink. It does not make its home in a plastic Solo cup.

2 ounces bourbon

◆

1 bar spoon rich simple syrup (2:1) (page 10)

◆

2 large sprigs of mint

Combine the syrup and one sprig of mint, composed of four or five leaves, at the bottom of a metal julep tin. Muddle gently. Add bourbon. Stir briefly and then add a cup of crushed ice. Stir for 15 seconds and add another cup of ice. Stir again until a frost develops on the outside of the tin. Add more ice, enough to form a dome of crushed ice above the cup's rim. Insert a metal spoon. Garnish with the second sprig of mint, placed near the straw, so that you get a whiff of its fragrance every time you lean in for a sip.

Grasshopper

You need a good crème to cacao, as well as a top-notch crème de menthe, for this drink to transcend the mediocre environs in which the Grasshopper typically dwells these days. Tempus Fugit's products will do you well. The problem with most modern, artisanal crème de menthes, however, is that many of them are clear, which robs the drink of the brilliant green hue that drinkers expect from a Grasshopper—an attribute that is, quite frankly, one of the drink's great attractions. But if it's a choice between color and taste, I'm going with taste.

1 ounce crème de menthe

1 ounce crème de cacao

1 ounce heavy cream

Freshly grated nutmeg

Combine all the ingredients except the grated nutmeg with ice in a cocktail shaker and shake vigorously until chilled and well integrated, about 15 seconds. Strain into a chilled coupe. Garnish with a dusting of grated nutmeg.

CHAMPAGNE COCKTAIL

There's no living down a name like "Champagne Cocktail." If a drink is called Champagne Cocktail, it's a fancy drink. That's all there is to it. There's Champagne in the glass and Champagne in the name. It's a high-toned tipple, and no question. Doesn't matter if it's composed of just a sugar cube, a few flecks of bitters, and some wine—an almost ridiculously simple recipe. Simplicity doesn't equal simple. There's not much to a little black dress, either, after all, but damn if it ain't sophisticated looking.

The Champagne Cocktail is so sleek and simple and elegant in profile that it almost seems wrong to call it a cocktail at all. But the name is accurate, and a cocktail, in both theory and soul, it is. In formula, it adheres to the old definition of the cocktail (liquor, bitters, sugar) as much as that ur-cocktail, the Old-Fashioned Whiskey Cocktail, but with wine used instead of spirit, and a flute instead of a rocks glass.

Though the drink feels utterly modern, like something F. Scott Fitzgerald might have sipped at in between dips in the Plaza Hotel fountain, the Champagne Cocktail is actually quite an old idea. The drink appeared in a book at its very first opportunity, in bartender Jerry Thomas's groundbreaking 1862 manual. Thomas kept it simple: wine, sugar, bitters, twist. Some bartenders between that year and the dawn of Prohibition in 1920 did what they could to tart the drink up, throwing mint, pineapple, strawberries, and all sorts of fruit in the glass. (In this way, too, the drink's history mirrors that of the Old-Fashioned, which got fruitier as it got older. One wonders whether the lobbyists from the American Fruit Company spent a lot of time hanging around bars.) But wisdom returned with Repeal, and the drink is generally served pretty simply in most bars.

And why not? Why reach for gaudy fruit when you've got that sugar cube in there, slowing dissolving, releasing a stream of fine bubbles and sweetness into the drink? This is a drink that comes with its own built-in fireworks.

champagne cocktail

Champagne, to top

◆

3 to 4 dashes Angostura bitters

◆

1 sugar cube

Lemon twist

Use a dry Champagne in this, well chilled.

Place the sugar cube at the bottom of a Champagne flute and saturate it with bitters. Slowly fill the glass with Champagne. Garnish with the lemon twist—the more ornamental, the better.

BRANDY ALEXANDER

In the early 1970s, John Lennon, on a break from his wife, Yoko Ono, dove head first into an infamous "lost weekend," bar-hopping with his close buddy, singer and gadabout Harry Nilsson, and generally making a lost-boys spectacle of himself. The spree reached its peak of notoriety in March 1974, when Lennon and Nilsson were thrown out of the Troubadour in Los Angeles, where the Smothers Brothers were performing. That night just happened to be the one when Nilsson, an accomplished drunk, introduced Lennon to the pleasures of the Brandy Alexander.

Lennon eventually returned to Ono, and his reputation rebounded. Nilsson's never quite did. "It still haunts me," Nilsson said in his final interview, before he died in 1994. "People think I'm an asshole and a mean guy. They still think I'm a rowdy bum from the 1970s who happened to get drunk with John Lennon, that's all. I drank because they did. I just introduced John and Ringo to Brandy Alexanders, that was my problem."

That was pretty much the last the world heard from the Brandy Alexander. It was hardly a handsome send-off for a drink that had once been both popular and respectable. Even as the twenty-first century dawned, and old cocktails were being regularly rescued from obscurity by missionary mixologists, it was difficult to find a Brandy Alexander on the menu at any upstanding cocktail den. Bartenders had bravely charged into the fast-collapsing, burning house that was the pre-Prohibition cocktail catalog to save the Aviation, the Last Word, the Brandy Crusta, the Martinez, and many more before they were lost forever. But when it came time to rescue the Brandy Alexander from that attic bedroom in the back and to the right, the bartenders collectively shrugged, muttered, "Screw it," and walked away. It wasn't worth it.

The Brandy Alexander wasn't alone. Most cream cocktails were judged as being beyond reclamation, including some rather good ones, like the Grasshopper. It was the one old category of cocktails that bartenders and drinkers just couldn't get excited about. Americans' habits had changed since the mid-twentieth century, when such after-dinner drinks still enjoyed a place at the table. People were eating and drinking lighter, or were trying to, anyway. And they avoided sweet drinks like the plague. The name Brandy Alexander telegraphed both "heavy" and "sweet" to most ears.

Though it's the brandy version we know best today, the Alexander cocktail began as a gin drink, making its first appearances in books in the years before Prohibition hit.

The drink had a fair amount of cred among the cultured classes once upon a time. Evelyn Waugh saw fit to have Anthony Blanch, the 1920s aesthete in his novel *Brideshead Revisited*, drink them—a fact fellow English author and drinking expert Kingsley Amis knew. Amis wrote that the drink was deceptively strong. But, then, he was accustomed to quadrupling the amount of brandy. The vain and imperious critic and columnist Alexander Woollcott reportedly thought enough of the drink to insist it had been named after him. Tennessee Williams, while writing *A Streetcar Named Desire* in New Orleans, would drink one daily and then swim fifteen lengths in the pool at the New Orleans Athletic Club—a practice I would not recommend for anyone other than a self-destructive genius.

The original gin drink is very good but lacks the fullness of flavor of the brandy version. In a Gin Alexander, it's the cream you taste, not the liquor. That's not the case with the brandy version. If you use a good, dry cognac, and a good crème de cacao, the Brandy Alexander is a very satisfying after-dinner quaff with a distinct spiritous edge. It is, as Stanley Clisby Arthur wrote in his *Famous New Orleans Drinks and How to Mix 'Em*, "Smooth as cream, delicate as dew and easily prepared."

Actually, Arthur wrote that about the gin version. Imagine what he would have written about the Brandy Alexander.

Brandy Alexander

There aren't many good crème de cacaos on the market; find the one made by Tempus Fugit, a distiller in California.

2 ounces cognac

1 ounce crème de cacao

1 ounce cream

Freshly grated nutmeg

Combine all the ingredients except the grated nutmeg with ice in a cocktail shaker and shake vigorously until chilled and well integrated, about 15 seconds. Strain into a chilled coupe. Garnish with a dusting of grated nutmeg.

white Russian

This rather unsubtle, postwar favorite was restored to relevancy by the Coen Brothers film *The Big Lebowski*, in which Jeff Bridges's sublimely unfazed Dude drinks them religiously. It's a good drink if you're not inclined toward a lot of thinking at the moment (which was just about any moment for the Dude). The vodka ensures it doesn't approach the flavor complexity of a Brandy Alexander. But if both vodka and cream and coffee are among your favorite things, this may be your jam.

1½ ounces vodka

¾ ounce Kahlúa

¾ ounce heavy cream

Combine all the ingredients in a cocktail shaker filled with ice and shake until chilled and well integrated, about 15 seconds. Strain into a chilled Old-Fashioned glass.

Acknowledgments

For their help and contributions, both big and small, I'd like to thank Talia Baiocchi, Deborah Berke, Julio Bermejo, Adam Bernbach, Jeff Berry, Greg Boehm, Jacob Briars, Jackson Cannon, Toby Cecchini, Meaghan Dorman, John Dye, Eben Freeman, Dan Greenbaum, Paul Harrington, Jason Kosmas, Brad Thomas Parsons, Del Pedro, Debbie Rizzo, Joaquín Simó, Nick Strangeway, Alan Sytsma, Sother Teague, David Wondrich, and Dushan Zaric. Special thanks to my agent David Black, for his constant help and guidance, and my smart and sane editor Emily Timberlake, who is ever a joy to work with and always "gets it." Greatest thanks, as always, to my teenage son, Asher. In not too many years, Asher, you'll be 21, and we'll finally be able to walk into a bar and laugh together over a drink about the weird way Dad makes a living. This will all make more sense in retrospect. I promise you.

About the Author

ROBERT SIMONSON writes about cocktails, spirits, bars, and bartenders for the *New York Times,* to which he has contributed since 2000. He is the author of *A Proper Drink* and *The Old-Fashioned,* and a contributor to *The Essential New York Times Book of Cocktails* and *Savoring Gotham.* His writings have appeared in *Saveur, Food & Wine, GQ, Lucky Peach, Whisky Advocate, Imbibe, Milwaukee Magazine,* and *Punch,* where he is a contributing editor. He is also coauthor of the cocktail app *Modern Classics of the Cocktail Renaissance.* A native of Wisconsin, he has lived in New York City since 1988.

Index